New Directions for
Adult and Continuing
Education

MW01274070

Susan Imel
Jovita M. Ross-Gordon
Joellen E. Coryell
COEDITORS-IN-CHIEF

Spirituality in the Workplace: A Philosophical and Social Justice Perspective

Marilyn Y. Byrd

EDITOR

Number 152 • Winter 2016
Jossey-Bass
San Francisco

Spirituality in the Workplace: A Philosophical and Social Justice Perspective
Marilyn Y. Byrd (ed.)
New Directions for Adult and Continuing Education, no. 152

Coeditors-in-Chief: *Susan Imel, Jovita M. Ross-Gordon, and Joellen E. Coryell*

NEW DIRECTIONS FOR ADULT AND CONTINUING EDUCATION, (Print ISSN: 1052-2891; Online ISSN: 1536-0717), is published quarterly by Wiley Subscription Services, Inc., a Wiley Company, 111 River St., Hoboken, NJ 07030-5774 USA.

Postmaster: Send all address changes to NEW DIRECTIONS FOR ADULT AND CONTINUING EDUCATION, John Wiley & Sons Inc., C/O The Sheridan Press, PO Box 465, Hanover, PA 17331 USA.

Copyright and Copying (in any format)

Information for subscribers

NEW DIRECTIONS FOR ADULT AND CONTINUING EDUCATION is published in 4 issues per year. Institutional subscription prices for 2017 are:

Print & Online: US$454 (US), US$507 (Canada & Mexico), US$554 (Rest of World), €363 (Europe), £285 (UK). Prices are exclusive of tax. Asia-Pacific GST, Canadian GST/HST and European VAT will be applied at the appropriate rates. For more information on current tax rates, please go to www.wileyonlinelibrary.com/tax-vat. The price includes online access to the current and all online back-files to January 1st 2013, where available. For other pricing options, including access information and terms and conditions, please visit www.wileyonlinelibrary.com/access.

Delivery Terms and Legal Title

Where the subscription price includes print issues and delivery is to the recipient's address, delivery terms are **Delivered at Place (DAP)**; the recipient is responsible for paying any import duty or taxes. Title to all issues transfers FOB our shipping point, freight prepaid. We will endeavour to fulfil claims for missing or damaged copies within six months of publication, within our reasonable discretion and subject to availability.

Back issues: Single issues from current and recent volumes are available at the current single issue price from cs-journals@wiley.com.

Disclaimer

Publisher: NEW DIRECTIONS FOR ADULT AND CONTINUING EDUCATION is published by Wiley Periodicals, Inc., 350 Main St., Malden, MA 02148-5020.

Journal Customer Services: For ordering information, claims and any enquiry concerning your journal subscription please go to www.wileycustomerhelp.com/ask or contact your nearest office.
Americas: Email: cs-journals@wiley.com; Tel: +1 781 388 8598 or +1 800 835 6770 (toll free in the USA & Canada).
Europe, Middle East and Africa: Email: cs-journals@wiley.com; Tel: +44 (0) 1865 778315.
Asia Pacific: Email: cs-journals@wiley.com; Tel: +65 6511 8000.
Japan: For Japanese speaking support, Email: cs-japan@wiley.com.
Visit our Online Customer Help available in 7 languages at www.wileycustomerhelp.com/ask

Production Editor: Poornita Jugran (email: pjugran@wiley.com).

View this journal online at wileyonlinelibrary.com/journal/ace

Wiley is a founding member of the UN-backed HINARI, AGORA, and OARE initiatives. They are now collectively known as Research4Life, making online scientific content available free or at nominal cost to researchers in developing countries. Please visit Wiley's Content Access - Corporate Citizenship site: http://www.wiley.com/WileyCDA/Section/id-390082.html

Printed in the USA by The Sheridan Group.

Address for Editorial Correspondence: Associate Editor, *Susan Imel, Jovita M. Ross-Gordon, and Joellen E. Coryell, NEW DIRECTIONS FOR ADULT AND CONTINUING EDUCATION,* Evmail: imel.l@osu.edu

Abstracting and Indexing Services

The Journal is indexed by Academic Search Alumni Edition (EBSCO Publishing); ERIC: Educational Resources Information Center (CSC); Higher Education Abstracts (Claremont Graduate University); Sociological Abstracts (ProQuest).

Cover design: Wiley
Cover Images: © Lava 4 images | Shutterstock

For submission instructions, subscription and all other information visit:
wileyonlinelibrary.com/journal/ace

CONTENTS

Editor's Notes

The trend toward spirituality in the workplace has emerged as more organizations and institutions have adopted a humanistic approach for creating fulfilling work environments (Garcia-Zamor, 2003). Spirituality is recognized as a conveyor or purpose in creating meaningful work and empowering people to achieve organizational goals (Gockel, 2004; Mitroff & Denton, 1999). Spirituality in the workplace has also been linked to fulfillment at work and its impact on the bottom line.

There has been a reasonable amount of literature from the field of education that speaks to the role of spirituality in teaching and learning (e.g., Dillard, Abdur-Rashid, & Tyson, 2000; English, 2000; Groen, 2005; Tolliver & Tisdell, 2006). The fields of social work and nursing have also made inroads for exploring how spirituality engages the beliefs of professionals (e.g., Grant, O'Neill, & Stephens, 2004; Matthews, 2009; McSherry, Cash, & Ross, 2004). But this is understandable given the humanistic nature of those helping professions.

In our work, we bring our authentic selves. Often, the authentic self is vulnerable to subjected to injustices derived from social identity designation or affiliation or from adverse, disempowering experiences that attack the soul. Therefore, perspectives of spirituality should consider ways that people engage in spirituality as a response to social injustice in the workplace. When work and the authentic self are in sync, work can be meaningful—a pathway to self-fulfillment and self-actualization (Maslow, 1968; Mathieson & Miree, 2003). But if the workplace becomes a site of social injustice, work and the authentic self are no longer in sync. People are then more likely to abandon individual pursuits in search of meaning-making responses to the injustice (Mathieson & Miree, 2003).

However, there is an absence of literature that has recognized spirituality as a force that creates energy to question, challenge, and reject systems of social injustice in the workplace. This volume seeks to create new discussions about spirituality and social justice in the context of the workplace. "Unless action is taken to contest prevailing systems in favor of justice, the unjust order will be strengthened and perpetuated" (Balasuriya, 1978, p. 2).

Chapter 1 explores how the meaning of work has changed in the contemporary workplace, hence creating a struggle for wholeness of self. Chapter 2 is a discussion of pedagogical strategies needed to transition learners from educational to organizational settings. Chapters 3 and 4 highlight spirituality in the narratives of women faculty of color who are often considered to be less competent or less knowledgeable than their counterparts in academic settings. Chapter 5 connects Indigenous philosophies of wholeness and the quest for a better world to principles of spirituality and social justice in workplaces and all places inhabited.

New Directions for Adult and Continuing Education, no. 152, Winter 2016 © 2016 Wiley Periodicals, Inc.
Published online in Wiley Online Library (wileyonlinelibrary.com) • DOI: 10.1002/ace.20207

Chapters 6 and 7 apply transformative learning theory (Mezirow, 1997) to spirituality and social justice in the workplace. Transformative learning theory illustrates how engaging in discourse with others similarly affected stimulates critical reflection for greater meaning-making opportunities. Chapter 8 introduces the enlightened revelation framework, an integrative model of spiritual liberation and a vehicle for social change in the workplace. An enlightened revelation conveys hope and empowerment for those who resist and take action against social injustice in the workplace.

Our overarching vision is that this volume will benefit the work of educators, researchers, scholars, practitioners, and consultants who are seeking ways to promote spiritually engaging workplaces that are not only values added and leadership centered but morally responsible with social justice education goals. When one's conscience cannot uphold injustice in workplaces or if one can no longer endure its sufferings, it is necessary to create a new space for spirituality in which contesting the injustice is a natural part of self-growth and fulfillment of purpose by a Higher Power (Balasuriya, 1978).

Marilyn Y. Byrd
Editor

References

Balasuriya, T. (1978). Towards a spirituality of social justice. *Logos, 17*(4), 1–5.

Dillard, C. B., Abdur-Rashid, D., & Tyson, C. A. (2000). My soul is a witness: Affirming pedagogies of the spirit. *International Journal of Qualitative Studies in Education (QSE), 13*(5), 447–462. doi:10.1080/09518390050156404

English, L. M. (2000). Spiritual dimensions of informal learning. In L. English & M. Gillen (Eds.), *New Directions for Adult and Continuing Education: No. 85. Addressing the spiritual dimensions of adult learning: what educators can do* pp. 29–38. San Francisco, CA: Jossey-Bass.

Garcia-Zamor, J. (2003). Workplace spirituality and organizational performance. *Public Administration Review, 63*(3), 355–363.

Gockel, A. (2004). The trend toward spirituality in the workplace: Overview and implications for career counseling. *Journal of Employment Counseling, 42*, 156–167.

Grant, D., O'Neil, K., & Stephens, L. (2004). Spirituality in the workplace: New empirical directions in the study of the sacred. *Sociology of Religion, 65*(3), 265–283.

Groen, J. (2005). Spirituality of adult education and training. *Studies in Continuing Education, 27*(1), 95–99.

Maslow, A. H. (1968). *Toward a psychology of being*. New York: D. Van Nostrand Company.

Mathieson, K., & Miree, C.E. (2003). Illuminating the invisible: IT and self-discovery in the work-place. In R. A. Giacalone & C. L. Jurkiewicz (Eds.), *Handbook of workplace spirituality and organizational performance* (pp. 461–474). Armonk, NY: M.E. Sharpe

Matthews, I. (2009). *Social work and spirituality*. Thousand Oaks: Sage.

McSherry, W., Cash, K., & Ross, L. (2004). Meaning of spirituality: Implications for nursing practice. *Journal of Clinical Nursing, 13*(8), 934–941. doi:10.1111/j.1365-2702.2004.01006.x

Mezirow, J. (1997). Transformative learning: Theory to practice. In P. Cranton (Ed.), *New Directions for Adult & Continuing Education: No. 74. Transformative learning in action: Insights from practice* (pp. 5–12). San Francisco, CA: Jossey-Bass.

Mitroff, I. I., & Denton, E. A. (1999). A study of spirituality in the workplace. *Sloan Management Review, 40*(4), 83–92.

Tolliver, D. E., & Tisdell, E. J. (2006). Engaging spirituality in the transformative higher education classroom. In E. W. Taylor (Ed.), *New Directions for Adult and Continuing Education No. 109. Teaching for change: Fostering transformative learning in the classroom* (pp. 37–47). San Francisco, CA: Jossey-Bass.

MARILYN Y. BYRD, PhD, is assistant professor of human relations, University of Oklahoma, Norman, OK.

1

The changing meaning of work calls for care and concern for the spiritual dimension of the workplace. Toward this end, a more liberal form of workforce education and human resource development in response to workplace preparation for managers is needed.

Spirituality as Foundation of Agency in Turbulent Economic Times

K. Peter Kuchinke

Be kind, for everyone you meet is fighting a great battle.

Ian McLaren, 1850–1907

Writing about spirituality invites, like few other dimension of adult and continuing education, reflection about one's own trajectory as well as a personal and conversational style of expression rather than the traditional analytic and detached form of writing. Markers of my own development, both private and professional, might be a commitment to the existential philosophies of Kierkegaard, Heidegger, and Sartre during early adulthood and professional training and qualification in psychological counseling approaches affiliated with the humanistic orientations of Rogers and Janov. The shift to a career in workforce and human resource education since the mid-1980s, as administrator, consultant, and university teacher, I was driven by the desire to be of use beyond the confines of the one-to-one clinical setting and to test what insights I may have gained in the wider world of work. An underlying theme of my scholarship in areas as disparate as leadership competencies, education of workforce trainers, and the changing meaning of work has been an interest in exploring the personal and inner dimensions of being at work. More precisely, a fascination is with the private selves at work, so often hidden behind the veil of the public persona, we enact our occupational roles in organizational and institutions. Questioning the demarcation between public and private selves, I have critiqued the functionalist reading of workforce education as insufficient for pragmatic and ethical reasons and instead positioned a liberal form of education as a much needed antidote (e.g., the critique of the business school preparation of modern managers (Kuchinke, 2007). Although instrumental and managerialist

New Directions for Adult and Continuing Education, no. 152, Winter 2016 © 2016 Wiley Periodicals, Inc.
Published online in Wiley Online Library (wileyonlinelibrary.com) • DOI: 10.1002/ace.20208

orientations are endemic to contemporary workforce and human resource education, and, sadly, the wider field of educational research and practice (for an excellent set of articles on the state of the humanities in education, see Higgins, 2015), care of and concern for the spiritual dimension of work and working should be seen as a central concern of adult, professional, and continuing education.

A second consideration in writing this chapter is the need for respect, perhaps even reverence, for the nature of the topic, the deep intellectual traditions of its foundations, and our own shortcomings and limitations. Here, I echo Kang's insightful essay on the need for humility in theorizing and practicing our craft: "Humility as a virtue in both the East and the West is characterized as embracing self-awareness about one's own capacities, exercising self-discipline and having a humanitarian orientation . . . . It is the recognition . . . of the limits of one's own virtues and talents" (Kang & Kuchinke, 2008, p. 5).

Although the growing interest in spirituality in many areas of educational practice is welcomed by many educators, mainstream corporate and neoliberal ideologies easily dismiss it as the idle obsession of starry-eyed academic idealists, who do not understand the real world of business anyhow (see e.g., Milton Friedman's [1970] wholesale dismissal of corporate social responsibility). Where spirituality does find acceptance, I observe the tendency toward commercialization and cheapening of what, in my understanding, is a dimension of human existence that eludes easy capture and instrumental use. Spiritual growth and development, in many wisdom traditions, are connected to notions such as blessings and grace, struggle and failure, longing, lifelong quest, and unknowing (e.g., Foster, 1988; Johnston, 1996; Loy, 1996). Based on this understanding, I view with concern the attempts to put spirituality to use in order to achieve exterior goals, to build it into the formal workforce education or corporate curriculum, or to create corporate cultures built on spirituality. The important lessons in life are learned and not taught, and the teacher will arrive only when the student is ready, as two old axioms go. To me, matters of spirituality are private and the role of the educator best described as the guide who, ever so gently, listens, supports, offers guidance when requested, and, perhaps foremost, leads through her own example in words and action. And yet, despite the private nature of spirituality, I welcome the rise of interest, publications, and research on the topic in educational and even workplace contexts. They are evocative reminders of the need for a holistic understanding of ourselves and of the interdependence of heart, head, and hands so well articulated in the cooperative education movement. They also suggest powerful ways to counter the tendency toward fragmentation and consumer-oriented nihilism in contemporary society and to strengthen the focus on humane education as a much-needed alternative to behaviorist-focused teaching and scholarship.

In this chapter, I try to articulate some perspectives as a scholar, teacher, and practitioner in workforce education and human resource development.

New Directions for Adult and Continuing Education • DOI: 10.1002/ace

The focus on inner dimensions of the self takes on particular salience in an educational field of practice that attempts the balancing act between performative dimensions and well-being and flourishing in workplace settings (Kuchinke, 2011) in what Fenwick (2011) has aptly described as our field's "dance with capital" (p. 88). I begin with a reflection on the state of the discussion in the professional community to show the range of approaches and considerations as exemplified at a recent annual meeting. I then explore the burgeoning interest in spirituality in a historical frame and then as related to conceptualizations of the role of work and career in today's society. Three ways of connecting spirituality and work are described, and I conclude with some thoughts on the role and responsibility of adult education and workforce and human resource development. Throughout, I refrain from attempts to bound, limit, or define the term, an effort beyond the scope of this chapter and undertaken elsewhere, not the least in the 2000 issue of this journal (English & Gillen, 2000). Instead, I simply refer interchangeably to the spiritual, inner, and personal dimensions of work, a stance taken in light of the thorny problem of capturing a holistic notion within the limits of language. I recognize further that spirituality, by whatever definition or approach, is not anything special or extra, but in fact part and parcel of our being, and that the struggle to realize deeper aspects of our being does, indeed, characterize every one of us, and thus Ian McLaren's aphorism at the beginning of this chapter.

Discourse of Spirituality in the Workplace

A starting point for this essay might be the symposium on spirituality at a recent national conference of the Academy of Human Resource Development (Abichandani, Alagaraja, & Ghosh, 2015). Although the topic had gained acceptance and even popularity over the past several years—some 25 conceptual and empirical conference papers have been presented since 2012— the 2015 session was the first focused event bringing together scholars from a variety of perspectives, persuasions, and cultural backgrounds. Panelists and participants addressed, in often highly personal style, their commitments, struggles, and hopes for an understanding and a practice of workforce and human resource education that was not fragmented and paid homage to the holistic nature of being in this world. The range of contributions was broad indeed. Several colleagues were quite comfortable exploring the utility of spirituality in the workplace in terms of individual-, group-, and organization-level outcomes and argued for operational definitions, measurement, and theory building. Some spoke of the need for conceptual clarification, whereas others still warned of the risks of normalization and instrumental use in the hands of business consultants, self-help book authors, and corporate executives, and others questioned if the private and sacred nature of spirituality could find a place in the rough and tumble of organizational life.

New Directions for Adult and Continuing Education • DOI: 10.1002/ace

Spiritual Dimensions and Work in Historical Context

A short foray into the historical understandings of the relationship between the spiritual dimension and work serves to show the context and time-bound nature of today's discussion and perspectives. Many authors have alluded to the hunger for connectedness and grounding in today's highly individualistic and fragmented society. Conger (1994), for example, notes the decline of traditional institutions, such as religious and civic organizations, and the increased expectation that employment settings provide meaning and belonging. Yet workplaces have become unstable institutions unable to provide sustained meaning and satisfaction of deeper needs. The *betrayal of modern work*, the subtitle of Joanne Ciulla's (2000) book, is a frequent theme in the sociology of work. Postmodern scholars speak of the untethering of meaning and identity from tradition in today's consumer-oriented society, a moment in history well characterized by Zygmunt Bauman's (2000) term of *liquid modernity*. In this context, a burgeoning literature positions spirituality and meaning as a personal resource to counter the vagaries of today's social and economic environment. Ambrose (2006), for example, invites readers to "find meaning in the madness [of work]" (p. 1) by exploring its mysteries and paradoxes and making peace with our work. Simplistic as this form of self-help advice may be, it points to a widely felt need grounded in the increased expectation of work as a source of spirituality.

Placher's (2005) analysis of the evolution of work and spiritual identity provides a historical perspective. Writing from a Christian perspective, he distinguished four historical periods. During the centuries preceding the Reformation in the early 16th century, spiritual growth and development were entirely separated from work and maximally connected to formal religion. Being called was seen as a particular form of spiritual expression and meant allegiance to the church in the early centuries. During the Middle Ages, it became associated with joining the clergy. The vocation of early Christians, the term derived from the Latin *vocare* meaning to name or to call, was divorced from any secular meaning, and the process of working not linked to spiritual identity or inner meaning. Not until the Reformation is there a link between work and religious or spiritual identity. "[Y]our job was your vocation, and thus everyone, not just priests, nuns, and monks, was called by God to their particular work" (Placher, 2005, p. 8). The critique of work under an emerging capitalist economic system, expressed in the Marxian notion of alienated labor and later in the critique of consumer-oriented society, tarnished the potential and promise of work as an expression of the individual's inner dimension. The hunger for deeper meaning in life and work appears as a consequence of the individualization and isolation of the spiritual dimension from the collective. It further signals a retreat of the spiritual dimension into the private domain, with a vacuum of inner meaning and spiritual dimension felt keenly in the harried, breathless, and shallow routines of much of contemporary work life.

New Directions for Adult and Continuing Education • DOI: 10.1002/ace

Spirituality and the Changing Nature of Work and Career

The resurging interest in meaning of work is a marker of the enduring nature of spirituality as a central human concern. The United States, for example, is among the most individualistic, fast-paced, and consumption-driven societies in the world but also ranks high in spirituality, whether this is measured by membership in organized religion, in private forms such as meditation, personal prayer, and yoga, or in the search for meaning in work. Many observers of contemporary work have noted the tension between the realities of everyday work and the dream of an integration or harmonization of the self and the workplace. This tension has become a significant characteristic of industrialized work and modern society. It is well expressed in the opening page of the best-selling book *Working*, which contains first-person narratives from individuals in a wide range of occupations:

> This book, being about work, is, by its very nature, about violence—to the spirit as well as to the body. It is about ulcers as well as accidents, about shouting matches as well as fistfights, about nervous breakdowns as well as kicking the dog around. It is, above all (or beneath all), about daily humiliations. To survive the day is triumph enough for the walking wounded among the great many of us. (Terkel, 2004, p. xi)

There is growing disenchantment with the possibilities and ethics of large organizational bureaucracies, be they U.S.-style multinational corporations, Korean family-owned *chebol*, or nongovernmental organizations of the United Nations. In the North American context, the philosophical tenets of quality management of the 1980s have given way to harsher employment regimes and the corporate landscape is now characterized by downsizing, restructuring, outsourcing, and offshoring of jobs. Work in modern organizations is described as increasingly complex, ambiguous, and uncertain (Baldry et al., 2007). This has altered the nexus between work and identity in the current volatile and shifting economic and societal moment where

> the catchword is flexibility, and this increasingly fashionable notion stands for a game of hire and fire with very few rules attached but with the power to change the rules unilaterally . . . [T]he prospect of constructing a lifelong identity on the foundation of work is, for the great majority of people, . . . dead and buried. (Bauman, 2006, pp. 316–317).

Career researchers, likewise, have noted a far-reaching change in how careers are constructed and enacted. Much attention has focused on the emergence of a new career pattern, promising to offer individual fulfillment, growth, and self-determination. The protean career model stands in sharp contrast to the traditional one that is governed by the demands and provisions of the employing organizations. Although there is little doubt that some individuals have been able to carve out their own niche and succeeded in re-making their careers in line with their talents, values, and desires, there is little evidence to suggest that this model holds true for a majority (Kuchinke, 2013).

The context in which careers are lived out in today's institutions and organizations is complex, dynamic, and contradictory. Benefits in the form of challenging assignments, intrinsic rewards, and fulfilling work occur to some individuals some of the time, but this is often accompanied by high levels of stress and personal sacrifices. Living and working on the edge is the norm for some, as was shared with me in an interview with a regional manager of a global pharmaceutical company in charge of human resource management for Europe, North Africa, and the Middle East: "When I stand on the shores of the Red Sea at night after a business meeting, I cannot believe the turn my life has taken after growing up in a small village in Germany. It even makes me forget my two divorces and the fact that my children don't want to talk to me any more" (personal communication, name withheld, September 25, 2007).

In light of far-reaching changes in the world of work and in career progression and patterns, empirical research on the meaning of work shows that individuals preserve the value of the personal and limit the extent of engagement or identification with work in countries around the world. In an international survey of white-collar employees in eight countries, Kuchinke (2011) reported that individuals tended to value involvement with family higher as a source of meaning and identity than engagement in work. Another survey, conducted by the German association of labor unions, found that a majority of German manufacturing employees gladly traded higher salaries and advancement at work for more personal time (Deutscher Gewerkschaftsbund, 2008). Based on these and many other studies, the wholesale colonialization of the private domain by corporate agendas predicted by critical scholars such as Deetz (1992) seems to have been countered by spirited assertions of the individual enacting firm boundaries between personal and work domains and, where possible, limiting time and energy involvement with work demands.

Spirituality and Work: Integration, Differentiation, or Fragmentation?

How, then, does spirituality, characterized by search and struggle for wholeness and belonging, inner peace and connectedness, fit with the complex, contradictory, and fast-paced nature of modern work and career? Three forms of fit might be considered. An integration perspective proposes unity and consistency, a differentiation perspective suggests tension and conflict, and a fragmentation perspective points to ambiguity and movement in and out of focus and clarity (see also Kuchinke, 2005).

The integration perspective assumes a harmonious relationship between spirituality and work, either actually achieved or at least potentially achievable given the right circumstances and sufficient energy and determination. Much of consultant-based and mass-marked business writing adopts this perspective. Here, work is portrayed as an extension of the self where inner values find outward expression, where spiritual growth and professional engagement are mutually reinforcing, and where the spiritual dimension of the self flows easily into work roles and activities. This concordance of the inner dimension of the person and work might have resulted from a struggle with adversity or a breakthrough in consciousness in form of a vision or inspiration.

The differentiation perspective, in contrast, denies the easy fit of spiritual growth and work. In this understanding, there exists conflict and contradiction between the work domain and the inner dimensions of the self, and this is due to the pressures of economic and organizational goals that constrain and even hinder spiritual development. As a result, compromise and compartmentalization are needed to cope. The segmentation of the self into inner and outer worlds might be experienced as natural in contemporary society or as a necessity that is accepted with regret. Role performance at work is guided by organizational mandates and objectives, and individuals contribute to corporate goals on the basis of their training, interests, and ambitions. Spiritual growth finds its place in the private sphere, such as family, friends, and spiritual community, shielded and protected from the pressures of daily work, and can serve as a source of rejuvenation and strength.

The fragmentation perspective removes the assumption of fit or balance and emphasizes, instead, multiplicity of meaning and discontinuity. The spiritual dimension, along with other central commitments and concerns, moves in and out of focus in the push and pull of competing endeavors and may even lose relevance in dark night of the soul. This perspective is aligned with the critique of the modernist agenda of progress, stability, and order. Even the search for authenticity, spiritual awareness, and agency become suspect and contaminated by attempts at domination by powerful institutions and ideologies (e.g., Deetz, 1992). As Martin (1992, p. 156) wrote:

> [A] fragmented self constantly fluctuates among diverse and changing identities, pulled by issues and events . . .The self is fragmented by a variety of nested, overlapping identities, external influences, and levels of consciousness: The perceiving subject, deluded by imagined notions of its unity and coherence, is in actuality split in such imponderable ways.

Conclusion

In this chapter, I have tried to reflect on the spiritual domain in the context of work. Starting with the observation of the strong and increasing interest in the topic among educators and in workforce education and human resource development circles, I have traced the changing historical understandings of the relationship between the inner dimension of the self and work roles and activities. For many centuries, the mundane activity of work and the spiritual realm of religion coexisted without intersecting. The Protestant reformation of the 16th century linked spiritual salvation to worldly endeavors in direct manner. The rise of capitalism, its early critique of alienated labor, and the recent disenchantment with modern work have put into question the ability of organizations to provide meaning and to still the hunger for spiritual growth and connectedness. Empirical research into the meaning of work and career provides clear evidence that individuals in countries around the world safeguard personal interests and commitments from the demands of work and work organizations wherever possible. The expressed preference for family and personal time over work and career indicates the importance of nonwork domains in the lives of individuals and counters the exclusive search for meaning and belonging through engagement with work.

In my own understanding, the three modes that were introduced to frame the relationship between self and work are ideal types that illustrate alternatives but rarely exist in pure form. Reflecting about my own life and career, I can see instances, periods, and circumstances where one or the other mode prevailed, while competing forms were often in the background. The search for meaning and spiritual growth has certainly been a constant theme over the years, but career, family, and other obligations have often overshadowed the ability to focus as much as needed or wanted. Thus, compromise and segmentation of life pursuits appeared reasonable, though the little voice in the background kept nagging and suggesting to search for better balance. The dark night of the soul, where everything is questioned and not much makes sense any longer, has certainly been no stranger, and the path back has involved the kindness and wisdom of friends, counselors, and mentors. In my work with students, clients, and colleagues alike, openings and invitations to explore deeper issues are never far away. With students, these teachable moments may be discussions over the direction and content of term papers and dissertation projects, reviewing career plans and choices, or trying to help with personal conflicts and difficulties. In organizational consulting, particularly around issues of leadership and culture, I am frequently struck with the depth and sincerity of reflection among leaders wanting to act on their values, behave in authentic manner, and create nurturing and sustainable structures and processes. At the same time, I observe the anguish and pain when competing demands, corporate politics, and economic pressures stand in the way of aspirations and goals. In my university service roles, the struggle to find solutions to governance and resource allocation, finally, offer further opportunities and openings to dig deeper and surface issues of meaning and spirit. Of note is that these deeper conversations often happen unplanned, in the hall way after meetings, over lunch, or after hours. Rare is the occasion when spiritual growth and development are on the formal agenda, and yet this dimension is never far from the surface. It seems of great importance to let the other set the pace and depth of discussion around these issues and never to push, prod, or proselytize. Matters of spirituality are private, sensitive, and tender. Even though spirituality is core to our being, there are vast differences in levels of awareness, willingness, and

New Directions for Adult and Continuing Education • DOI: 10.1002/ace

ability to tend to this dimension and address them in the course of work and education.

Many come to workforce and human resource development by way of counseling, religious training, social work, and other areas of human care and concern. As educators we have the opportunity and privilege to address in our work the search for wholeness and care for the spiritual dimensions in ourselves and those whose lives we touch in our work. Education, as many progressive educators have noted, is about the whole person, and not separate facets, and in this vein it should be welcomed that the focus on spirituality is receiving greater attention in the research, writing, and practice in our various domains of practical involvement.

References

Abichandani, Y., Alagaraja, M., & Ghosh, R. (2015). Foundations of Indian spirituality in HRD research and practice. In J. Moats (Ed.), *Proceedings of the 2015 AHRD Conference of the Americas*. Session 40. St. Paul, MN: Academy of Human Resource Development.

Ambrose, D. (2006). *Making peace with your work: An invitation to find meaning in the madness.* Andover, MN: Expert Publishing.

Baldry, C., Bain, P., Taylor, P., Hyman, J., Scholarios, D., Marks, A., ... Bunzel, D. (2007) *The meaning of work in the new economy*, New York, NY: Palgrave/Macmillan.

Bauman, Z. (2000). *Liquid modernity*. Malden, MA: Blackwell.

Bauman, Z. (2006). On globalization: Or globalization for some, localization for some others. In P. Beilharz (Ed.), *The Bauman reader* (pp. 298–310). Oxford, UK: Blackwell.

Conger, J. A. (1994). *Spirit at work: Discovering the spirituality in leadership*. San Francisco, CA: Jossey-Bass.

Ciulla, J. B. (2000). *The working life: The promise and betrayal of modern work*. New York, NY: Three Rivers.

Deetz, S. (1992). *Democracy in an age of corporate colonialization: Developments in communication and the politics of everyday life*, Albany, NY: State University of New York.

Deutscher Gewerkschaftsbund. (2008). *DGB-index gute arbeit 2008. Wie die beschäftigten die arbeitswelt beurteilen, was sie sich von einer guten arbeit erwarten* [DGB-index good work 2008. How the employees assess the working environment, what do they expect of good work]. Retrieved from http://www.dgb-index-gute-arbeit.de

English, L. M., & Gillen, M. A. (2000). Editors' notes. In L. M. English & M. A. Gillen (Eds.), *New Directions for Adult and Continuing Education: No. 85. Addressing the spiritual dimensions of adult learning: What educators can do* (pp. 1–5). San Francisco, CA: Jossey-Bass.

Fenwick, T. (2011). Developing who, for what? Notes of caution in rethinking a global H(R)D: A response to Kuchinke. *Human Resource Development International, 14*(1), 83–89.

Foster, R. J. (1988). *Celebration of discipline: The path to spiritual growth*. San Francisco, CA: Harper-Collins.

Friedman, M. (1970, September 13). The social responsibility of business is to increase its profits. Retrieved from http://umich.edu/~thecore/doc/Friedman.pdf

Higgins, C. (Ed.). (2015). Humane education: Recovering the humanistic dimension of teaching, learning, and research. [Special issue]. *Educational Theory, 65*(6).

Johnston, W. (Ed.). (1996). *The cloud of unknowing*. New York, NY: Doubleday.

Kang, H. S., & Kuchinke, K. P. (2008, November). Humility in human resource development. In *Proceedings of the Academy of Human Resource Development in Asian Chapter Conference in Bangkok, Thailand*.

Kuchinke, K. P. (2005). The self at work: Theories about persons, the meaning of work, and their implications for HRD. In S. Turnbull & C. Elliott (Eds.), *Critical thinking in HRD* (pp. 141–155). London, UK: Routledge.

Kuchinke, K. P. (2007). Birds of a feather? The critique of the North American business school and its implications for educating HRD practitioners. *Human Resource Development Review*, 6(2), 111–126.

Kuchinke, K. P. (2011). Human flourishing as a core value for HRD in an age of global mobility. In M. Lee (Ed.), *HRD as we know it: Speeches that have shaped and developed the field of HRD* (pp. 292–305). London, UK: Routledge.

Kuchinke, K. P. (2013). Boundaryless and protean careers in a knowledge economy. In C. Valentin and J. Walton (Eds.), *Human resource development: Practices and orthodoxies* (pp. 202–221). Houndmills, Basingstoke, Hampshire, UK: Palgrave Macmillan.

Loy, D. (1996). *Lack and transcendence: The problem of death and life in psychotherapy, existentialism, and Buddhism*. Amherst, NH: Humanity.

Martin, J. (1992). *Cultures in organizations: Three perspectives*. Oxford, UK: Oxford University.

Placher, W. C. (2005). *Callings: Twenty centuries of Christian wisdom on vocation*. Grand Rapids, MI: William B. Eerdmans.

Terkel, S. (2004). *Working: People talk about what they do all day and how they feel about what they do*. New York, NY: New Press.

K. PETER KUCHINKE, PhD, is professor and director of graduate studies in the Department of Education Policy, Organization, and Leadership at the University of Illinois at Urbana-Champaign.

New Directions for Adult and Continuing Education • DOI: 10.1002/ace

2

This chapter proposes a spiritually relevant and social justice pedagogy that assists learners in making the transition to the workplace. Key elements of this spirituality include religion, cultural diversity, identity, health, and social class. Pedagogical strategies for infusing this spirituality in the curriculum are given.

Social Justice and Spirituality: Educating for a Complicated Workplace

Leona M. English, Paula Cameron

In this 21st century world, it is not uncommon to hear that learners, educators, and employees are searching for some sense of meaning or purpose, especially in their work lives (e.g., Palmer, 2000). As educators in higher education, we are often challenged to think of how we can help in this existential search; indeed, we are on a similar quest to find meaning in our own vocation. We are aware that some of our colleagues in adult education see this challenge as revolving around questions of reflective practice (Hunt, 2009), others on the value of mindfulness and Jungian psychology (Cranton, 2006; Dirkx, 2013), some on how to be transformed in heart and mind (Cameron, 2014; Cranton, 2006), and yet others on questions of spirituality (English & Tisdell, 2010; Groen, Coholic, & Graham, 2012). In this chapter, we side with the latter group in framing our discussion in the language of spirituality of work, and we look for critical components of spirituality that make it a force for engaging issues of diversity, ethnicity, and gender. We begin with a discussion of the place of spirituality in the workplace and higher education. Then we move to a discussion of what we propose are the main elements of a critically engaged spirituality of adult education. Finally, we discuss how an adult educator in higher education can support the development of this social justice initiative.

The Context and the Challenges

Those of us who take on the task of adult education through the lens of spirituality have grown in number over the past decade and we have been engaged in a common quest to integrate spiritual searching into our conversations. In an effort not to ruffle feathers with colleagues, we have often spoken in soft terms about spirituality. Writers such as Tisdell (2003) describe spirituality

New Directions for Adult and Continuing Education, no. 152, Winter 2016 © 2016 Wiley Periodicals, Inc.
Published online in Wiley Online Library (wileyonlinelibrary.com) • DOI: 10.1002/ace.20209

as "an awareness and honoring of wholeness and the interconnectedness of all things through the mystery of ... Life-force, God, higher power, higher self, cosmic energy, Buddha nature or Great Spirit" (p. 28). Similarly, English and Gillen (2000) see spirituality as "an awareness of something greater than ourselves [... that] moves one outward to others as an expression of one's spiritual experiences" (p. 1). We have been complicit in erring on the soft and palatable version of spirituality in an effort to bring it into our classes, recognize its importance in our lives, and see it as part of meaning-making in our work. Of prime importance, has been our cardinal rule: to avoid religion in our discussion and to focus on the middle ground through the use of terms such as spirituality, meaning, wholeness, and searching. So soft and light has been our discussion that critical adult educators such as Mike Newman (2012) have basically scoffed at the idea of spirituality and adult education. We suspect he is not the only one, perhaps in part because it does not appear to connect to the critical concerns of adult education: race, class, gender, and identity.

Meanwhile, scholars writing in theology and religious studies, especially those with a sociological bent, have long seen the links between and among spirituality, religion and life's complexities, and have written about this at length (e.g., Chittister, 2008; Rolheiser, 2006). This conversation has been kept at a distance in adult education, to the point where the decennial *Handbook of Adult and Continuing Education* no longer includes a dedicated chapter on religious education, preferring the more benign discussion of spirituality (English & Tisdell, 2010). Ironically, nothing could be closer to our field than discussions about the religious impulses and supports for social change over the years. Many in our field, such as Yeaxlee (1925), one our first writers, had roots in faith-based organizations like the YMCA. The field has eschewed this link over time in an effort to cleanse the spiritual.

Meanwhile, after a long gap, at the turn of the 21st century adult education allowed considerable discussion of spirituality (Tisdell, 2003). Those engaged in teaching and researching at the higher education level have engaged spiritual language and texts as they provide professional and continuing professional education to help students think deeper and more critically about issues that confront the world, its peoples, and its complexity. Given the context of higher education, and the pressure to avoid conflict, to keep things smooth, many choose to present a palatable version of the topic that admits of no real essence or view on spirituality. Although issues of race, class, and gender may be on an adult education agenda, a critical spirituality or discussion of religion has by and large been a taboo in academe.

Lately some cognate areas have acknowledged the legitimacy of a discussion of religion, if only to point out that religion often is a force in women's lives globally (see Manicom & Walters, 2012). For instance, a recent special issue of the *Feminist Review* focused on the intersection of religion in the lives of women worldwide. Similarly, the *Canadian Journal of Development Studies* dedicated a special issue to this topic, signaling that religion is a factor in development that cannot be ignored. The Association of Women in

Development (AWID) makes clear that avoiding discussions of religion is a luxury of the West. They point to the fact that religion and religious fundamentalism, in particular, can control women's freedom, education, and access to a sustainable livelihood and as result must be included. In fact, AWID's research shows that 69% of activists from 160 countries surveyed "believe religious fundamentalisms obstruct women's rights more than other political forces" (Gokal, Barbero, & Balchin, 2011, p. 5). Given statistics like this, we have no choice but to reengage with the hard questions around religion/spirituality. Indeed, to refuse to acknowledge this element of difference is to pretend it does not exist, which begs the question of how we address issues that we cannot even name.

Global links and worldview are especially important to our field, which is oriented to justice for all, everywhere. Adult educators need to be mindful of these global links and of our responsibility to not forget these links and relationships. This necessarily involves understanding our often conflicted relationship to religious organizations and beliefs, created as they are by culture, society, and families of origin. Those who educate professionals to work in nonprofit organizations with immigrant groups, for instance, need to be very aware of religious and spiritual practices that are an integral part of an employee's life: think of fasting, Ramadan, prayer, and dietary needs. They may also need to challenge the all-too-common equation of religion with oppression, illiteracy, and female inequity.

Those engaged in workplace spirituality are in a similar bind, wanting to allow for spirituality, creativity, and reflection but not wanting to complicate it with crucial issues of justice. After all, the goal of such programming in a workplace is generally geared to compliance, rather than criticality, tied as it is to the bottom line. Workplace spirituality has often been tied to productivity and human resources, given the neoliberal agenda that tends to predominate in Western capitalist society (English & Mayo, 2012). It is not uncommon to hear of workplaces with yoga, retreats, meditation, and other initiatives designed to increase worker happiness. We are reminded that these are, by and large, dedicated to the bottom line, an increase in happiness or lower stress presumably leading to higher productivity. We are also aware that there is an emergent postcolonial critique of these kinds of practices (see Darroch, 2009). Under the guise of supporting and facilitating happiness, the workplace can advance a neocolonial agenda, though we might never label it as such.

Much of what passes for spirituality in the workplace is linked to a neoliberal attempt to colonize the spiritual and the emotional sphere of the worker. Similar to Hochschild's (1983) research on how some occupational groups, specifically service workers such as flight attendants and call center workers, are implicitly expected to perform untold amounts of emotional labor, it is clear that many workplace educators are being asked to do the same with the onset of integration of spirituality into the workplace, without context and without transparency. Workplace educators need to be careful to identity this neoliberal agenda (Gallagher, 2014) that can pervade these attempts and that

New Directions for Adult and Continuing Education • DOI: 10.1002/ace

end in asking employees to carry even more of an emotional burden, asking them to surrender their souls. As Hochschild pointed out, women have traditionally been tasked with a greater burden of emotional labor than their male counterparts. Colonizing the emotional life (smoothing over negative emotion) is an infringement that Western society has allowed to slip in.

The Critical Components

Rife as the everyday workplace is with conflict, stress, and issues of race, diversity, and sexism, it seems likely that a spirituality that can inform it has to be grounded in key social justice concerns. Confining spirituality to the pursuit of personal bliss is to support compliance and banality. An alternative is to admit of several possible components or dimensions of a bona fide spirituality.

Religion. Paulo Freire (1970), who stands tall in our field as a person informed by faith and close links to his religious tradition, never shied away from the critical questions facing learners and teachers (Boyd, 2012). His insights and his everyday way of engaging difference, inspired by his religious convictions, is key in this discussion. Freire allowed this religious impulse to inform his understanding of his role in education, most especially in his way of speaking back to power. Though religion may not be important for everyone, it might be useful to recognize it as a possible component of spirituality. Allowing for this possibility, instead of ignoring it, makes dialogue possible about issues of religious difference, as well as culture and practice. Such recognition helps us avoid essentialism, for example, labelling all Muslim or Christian women as the same, assuming they are replicas of each other, with no distinction between them. Similarly, Pui-lan (2005, 2010) reminds us, there is no single homogenous religion, whether it be Christianity, Islam, or Hinduism, as their concepts and practices have borrowed greatly from each other and from indigenous traditions. A critical adult educator needs to be aware that there are many ways to perform religion in everyday life and in the workplace—refusing to allow for this dimension limits the possibility of intercultural dialogue. In the same way that we have moved beyond the conversations on essentializing women as learners engendered by *Women's Ways of Knowing* (Belenky, Clinchy, Goldberger, & Tarule, 1986), we need to move beyond essentializing women of religious and spiritual commitments.

Cultural Diversity. A spirituality that is about transformation and meaning-making, that sees everyone's journey as the same is one that misses the complexities (and interesting components) of life. In addition to a spirituality that allows us to search inside ourselves, we might channel spirituality to embrace the ways that we are culturally different. In Nova Scotia, for instance, many community groups and not-for-profit agencies have deliberately and politically begun to acknowledge that they stand on Mi'kmaq Territory, the First Nations who were displaced by European settlers in the early 18th century. This is often done by asking an elder to lead the gathering (conference, banquet, and class) in a blessing that may be accompanied by a smudging ceremony. Though a small step forward, acknowledging Mi'kmaq rights publicly through their own religious ceremonies places a wedge in the complacency of settlers and facilitates conversations about the land, its peoples, and its many inhabitants. This conversation allows for and highlights the possibilities for difference, and advances the causes of various groups in a peaceful way. Similarly, many indigenous, indeed many cultural groups, observe numerous rituals and other practices when they experience sickness and death of a family member. It is expected that community members prepare food and participate in ceremonies, which are lengthy and which may conflict with workplace commitments and expectations. Similarly, many Muslims pray five times a day—naming this and appreciating it in scheduling to accommodate it in a workplace makes common sense.

Identity. When we allow for a spirituality that embraces challenges, issues and difference, we are inviting the active participation of marginalized groups and allowing for a diversity of expression and resistance in traditional space. The underground church of lesbian, gay, bisexual, trans*, or queer (LGBTQ) members in Jamaica is an example of resistance to organized religion and cultural norms in that country. This church works with participants, colleagues, and populations in Jamaica who identify as LGBTQ in order to assure their safety and their right to practice in congregations (Chisholm, 2013). Although they may technically be welcome in all churches, many do not feel included, making this underground church necessary, especially because issues such as how one identifies (male, female, nonbinary, and other) may be intricately connected to one's spirituality; gender identification and sexual attraction are core aspects of identity and an advanced understanding of spirituality and a welcoming spiritual community are needed. Similarly, Bryant, Isaac-Savage, and Bowman (2014) have highlighted how spirituality and religion can be core elements of identity for Black men. Our adult education conversations need to embrace and acknowledge varied aspects of identity.

Health. Spirituality is ultimately about our sense of well-being, the ability to move in the world in ways that give us quality of life and that allow for that sense while living in community. Spirituality in the workplace must move beyond discussions of bliss and uncomplicated livelihoods and deal with issues of wellbeing. Indeed, the equation of spirituality with the search for personal bliss is problematic as bliss is usually not moored to notions of responsibility or commitment to the other and ignores the reality of human suffering, which can also be the location of authentic spirituality. Without an anchor in the ebbs and flows of daily life, something the great spiritual writers such as Chittister (2008) attend to, we do not have a bona fide spirituality. Spirituality grounded in the full range of emotions and states of health may in fact be the source and sustenance we need to negotiate mental health issues, problems with colleagues, and conflict in general. Religious and spiritual traditions may be an integral part of healing and restoration.

Social Class. How spirituality is enacted and practiced is inevitably bound up in our own social class and that of our learners. Whereas, for some, spirituality finds expression in extended retreats and nature walks such as travelling across the Atlantic Ocean to walk the Camino de Santiago in Spain, for others it may be enhanced by a hike in a local park. When Dirkx (2013) talks about spirituality of work "as meaningful and purposeful," and of those who are "experiencing work as a sense of vocation or calling" (p. 359), we wonder if this is what a woman in South African townships thinks about. Often these expressions of spirituality are affected by one's financial location, both at present and through our family history. In each case, the rituals and socialization of family and friends affect how one enacts spirituality. Exposure to atheism and extended critiques of religion from writers such as Richard Dawkins (2009) likely increase with our literacy level and our access to public broadcasters and time to go to a library. Adult education, a field deeply embedded in social justice and community concerns, needs to be mindful of the ways in which it brings a middle class set of expectations to bear on discussions and understandings of spirituality.

Enhancing Spirituality in Adult Education

Knowing that spirituality needs a social justice and critical edge is just the beginning. Integrating these notions of critique into teaching and making the link to the world of work is more challenging. Yet, there are several strategies that we see as important to integrating a social justice spirituality into an adult education curriculum whether it be in formal, nonformal, or informal contexts. We suggest these strategies, knowing that education exists primarily in a neoliberal context in the West and making any changes that challenge the system can be difficult.

Asking Questions. Like Rilke (1984), we have come to "love the questions themselves" (p. 34), and agree that one of our primary tasks of an educators is to encourage similar questions in learners. For instance, one of us recently had a student propose an action research project to bring a spirituality program into a tired human resources department in local government. We asked the student to think about the purpose of the program, how much emotional labor it might call on from employees, who the program really benefitted, and who actually proposed the program. In light of these questions, the student was unable to justify the program to herself, so she set it aside. Our task as adult educators is to keep bringing forward questions that challenge Western, neoliberal workplaces, and the employees' place in them.

Challenging Assumptions. Assumptions about spirituality do indeed have to be examined in higher education and in the workplace. One key assumption is that spirituality is primarily concerned with the endless pursuit of happiness. Barbara Ehrenreich (2009) reminds us that there is something inherently destructive about a quest for happiness that does not acknowledge responsibility and that does not leave room for the downside and problems. She asks us to challenge assumptions about the fulfillment in the endless pursuit of positivity. Connecting this to the learners' and educators' search for spiritual bliss, we would add that looking on the bright side ignores the reality that spirituality can be tied intricately to mental health challenges, boredom, downturns, lost dreams, and transitions. Assumptions about spirituality that are not linked to reality and to the everyday complexities of human existence are to be challenged. As educators, we need to keep challenging the given and helping learners find alternatives. In our classes and in other learning situations, we have the responsibility of examining these assumptions and helping students to talk back to power.

Linking to Work. Many citizens were raised with the notion that school and work were two separate entities and that school was essentially preparation for life but not life itself. All too familiar is the idea that those who teach in higher education are located in an ivory tower that avoids the nitty-gritty of the workplace. Yet, a spirituality of lifelong learning includes work in a variety of settings. Wherever we are, school or work, spirituality is informed by our activity and vice versa. In the words of Matthew Fox (1994), this spirituality anchors us and keeps us from being "more worked than working" (p. 45). He encourages letting "interiority turn into effective action and effective action lead back to interiority" (p. 45). A focus on spirituality in higher education is not radically different from how it might be in the for-profit workplace. In recognizing and affirming that spirituality is part of this work in the here and now, and that this spirituality is full of difficult questions and challenges, learners will be better prepared to bring their questions and concerns to the workplace.

Linking to the Global Context. Travel and exposure to many cultures, ways of life, and differences are obvious ways to become deeply aware of the diversity of ways that spiritualty and social justice intersect. Equally important to travel is connecting an understanding of adult education in our own location to those in the global context. Although personal integration and individual transformation, for instance, are important aspects of adult education, we need always to relate these to global concerns and issues that stretch us and also help us think of how interconnected our global family is. Learning and analyzing policies such as the Millennium Development Goals and the CONFINTEA declarations help adult educators see how practices and beliefs in the West are united with universal concerns about primary education, lifelong learning, and barriers to participation (English & Irving, 2015). As adult educators, we might be engaged with AWID and its discussions about how women are affected by religious fundamentalism. A narrowly focused understanding of adult education cannot help us see the bigger picture and it can limit the possibilities for our discussion.

Conclusion

In summary, this chapter is about reclaiming a robust spirituality that is more in line with the social justice-infused spirituality that Freire promoted (Boyd, 2012). It is a spirituality that engages with difficult questions and global issues, which refuses to remain limited to individual growth and potential. This is a spirituality that has several main components, including the possibility of religious ties, ethnicity, race, and gender. This is critically infused spirituality that embraces life's complexity and allows for bliss as well as issues of depression, boredom, and failure. As spiritual writers such as Rolheiser (2006), Chittister (2008), and Palmer (2000) have noted, spiritualty is best viewed as entangled in real life concerns and not a place where one goes to avoid them. In teaching, we need to recognize that spirituality courses through our discourse—conversations and practices— and does not stand apart from it. Finally, an authentic spiritualty of adult education works in conversation with international adult education and global conversations about meaning and value and challenges inauthentic expression.

References

Belenky, M., Clinchy, B., Goldberger, N. R., & Tarule, J. (1986). *Women's ways of knowing: The development of self, mind, and voice.* New York, NY: Basic Books.

Boyd, D. (2012). Spirituality of Paulo Freire. *International Journal of Lifelong Education, 31*(6), 759–778. doi:10.1080/02601370.2012.723051.

Bryant, L. O., Isaac-Savage, E. P., & Bowman, L. (2014). Reflections on the spirituality of three black gay men. In Proceedings of the Adult Education Research Conference. Retrieved from http://newprairiepress.org/cgi/viewcontent.cgi?article=3287& context=aerc

Cameron, P. S. (2014). Learning with a curve: Young women's "depression" as transformative learning. In V. Wang (Ed.), *Handbook of research on adult and community health education: Tools, trends, and methodologies: Tools, trends, and methodologies* (pp. 100–122). Hershey, PA: IGI Global.

Chisholm, M. E. (2013). Let them be free: Adult education in an underground LGBT church in Jamaica. Proceedings of the Adult Education Research Conference. Retrieved from http://newprairiepress.org/cgi/viewcontent.cgi?article=2995&context=aerc

Chittister, J. (2008). *Joan Chittister: In my own words* (M. L. Kownacki, Comp. & Ed.). Ligouri, MI: Ligouri Publications.

Cranton, P. (2006). *Understanding and promoting transformative learning: A guide for educators of adults.* San Francisco, CA: Jossey-Bass.

Darroch, F. (2009). *Memory and myth: Postcolonial religion in contemporary Guyanese fiction and poetry.* Amsterdam, Holland; New York, NY: Rodopi.

Dawkins, R. (2009). *The god delusion.* New York, NY: Random House.

Dirkx, J. M. (2013). Leaning in and leaning back at the same time: Toward a spirituality of work-related learning. *Advances in Developing Human Resources, 15*(4), 356–369. DOI: 10.1177/1523422313498562

Ehrenreich, B. (2009). *Bright-sided: How the relentless promotion of positive thinking has undermined America.* New York, NY: Metropolitan Books.

English, L. M., & Gillen, M. A. (Eds.). (2000). Introduction. In L. M. English & M. A. Gillen (Eds.), *New Directions for Adult and Continuing Education: No. 85. Addressing the spiritual dimensions of adult learning* (pp. 1–3). San Francisco, CA: Jossey-Bass.

English, L. M., & Irving, C. (2015). Feminism and adult education: The nexus of policy, practice, and payment. *Canadian Journal for the Study of Adult Education, 27*(2), 16–30.

English, L. M., & Mayo, P. (2012). *Learning with adults: A critical pedagogical introduction.* Rotterdam, Holland: Sense Publishers.

English, L. M., & Tisdell, E. J. (2010). Spirituality and adult education. In C. E. Kasworm, A. D. Rose, & J. M. Ross-Gordon (Eds.), *Handbook of adult and continuing education* (pp. 285–293). Thousand Oaks, CA: Sage.

Fox, M. (1994). *The reinvention of work: A new vision of livelihood for our time*. San Francisco, CA: Harper.

Freire, P. (1970). *Pedagogy of the oppressed*. New York, NY: Continuum.

Gallagher, P. X. (2014). *Spirituality in the workplace: A study guide for business leaders*. TruthIn-Writing Group. Kindle books.

Gokal, S., Barbero, R., & Balchin, C. (Eds.). (2011). *Key learnings from feminists on the frontline: Summaries of case studies on resisting and challenging fundamentalisms*. Toronto, Canada; Mexico City, Mexico; Capetown, South Africa: Association of Women in Development. Retrieved from http://www.awid.org/publications/feminists-frontline-case-studies-resisting-and-challenging-fundamentalisms

Groen, J., Coholic, D., & Graham, J. R. (Eds.). (2012). Introduction. In *Spirituality in education and social work: Theory, practice and pedagogies* (pp. 1–13). Waterloo, ON, Canada: Wilfrid Laurier University Press.

Hochschild, A. (1983). *The managed heart: The commercialization of human feeling*. Berkeley, CA: University of California Press.

Hunt, C. (2009). A long and winding road: A personal journey from community education to spirituality via reflective practice. *International Journal of Lifelong Education, 28*(1), 71–89.

Manicom, L., & Walters, S. (Eds.). (2012). *Feminist popular education in transnational debates: Building pedagogies of possibility*. New York, NY: Palgrave Macmillan.

Newman, M. (2012). Calling transformative learning into question: Some mutinous thoughts. *Adult Education Quarterly, 62*(1), 36–55.

Palmer, P. (2000). *Let your life speak: Listening for the voice of vocation*. San Francisco, CA: Jossey- Bass.

Pui-lan, K. (2005). *Postcolonial imagination and feminist theology*. Louisville, KY: Westminster John Knox Press.

Pui-lan, K. (Ed.). (2010). *Hope abundant: Third world and indigenous women's theology*. Maryknoll, NY: Orbis Books.

Rilke, R. M. (1984). *Letter 4, Letters to a young poet*. (Trans. S. Mitchell). New York, NY: New Work House.

Rolheiser, R. (Ed.). (2006). *Secularity and the Gospel: Being missionaries to our children*. New York, NY: Crossroad Publishing.

Tisdell, E. J. (2003). *Exploring spirituality and culture in adult and higher education*. San Francisco, CA: Jossey-Bass.

Yeaxlee, B. (1925). *Spiritual values in adult education* (Vols. 1–2). New York, NY: Oxford University Press.

LEONA M. ENGLISH, *PhD, is a professor of adult education at St. Francis Xavier University, Antigonish, Nova Scotia, Canada.*

PAULA CAMERON, *PhD, is an assistant professor of adult education at St. Francis Xavier University, Antigonish, Nova Scotia, Canada.*

3

This chapter explores how both historically and in contemporary times of escalating violence against our bodies, minds, and spirits worldwide, Black women lead, love, and live *within contexts of suffering.*

To Address Suffering That the Majority Can't See: Lessons from Black Women's Leadership in the Workplace

Cynthia B. Dillard

Since our brutal arrival on these shores through the transatlantic slave trade, Black women have understood and experienced constant and continual oppression in the U.S. context and around the globe. Important and instructive from this experience is to understand the ways in which Black women also resiliently and brilliantly continue to love and lead. In this chapter, I use a narrative of my experience as a Black woman administrator in higher education to illustrate the ways we feel, suffer, and still make a way through the suffering for ourselves and in honor of countless others on whose shoulders we stand. For those who seek to center their work in spaces that embody and produce diversity, equity, and justice, understanding these sufferings is an important step to truly standing in solidarity with Black women as we articulate suffering and declare our sovereign right to love as our work ethic and to carry out our leadership in service to communities of affiliation and care.

It's All About Love

This chapter is all about love. And I speak here of the declarations of love that center and affirm that Black life matters and that loving Blackness is a sovereign place—maybe the *only* place—from which Black people can live fully. Many of us read for the first time a definition of love in bell hooks' (2000) book *All about Love*. This definition of love was actually put forth decades before by M. Scott Peck in *The Road Less Travelled* (1978). He said this:

> Love is the will to extend one's self for the purpose of nurturing one's own or another's spiritual growth . . . Love is as love does. Love is an act of will—namely

New Directions for Adult and Continuing Education, no. 152, Winter 2016 © 2016 Wiley Periodicals, Inc.
Published online in Wiley Online Library (wileyonlinelibrary.com) • DOI: 10.1002/ace.20210

an intention and an action. Will implies choice. We do not have to love. We
choose to love... (pp. 4–5)

hooks (2000) then extended Peck's discussion to talk about the ingredi-
ents of love: care, affection, recognition, respect, commitment, trust, and honest and open communication. In earlier work, I've marshaled the idea that,
despite the evidence all around us (seen and unseen), Black women marshal
the social, cultural, and spiritual strength to make these declarations of love every day all day, to make declarations of the goodness of our existence (Dillard,
2012; Dillard & Okpalaoka, 2011). Even as we are disregarded by others, we
can also choose to be and think from an endarkened epistemology that makes
a sovereign claim and recognition of our worthiness (Dillard, 2006). We form
these spaces and places of recognition and love and hope that *declare* that
our lives matter. But, as with any work that focuses on endarkening our epis-
temologies (i.e., in making sense of our lives against a Black backdrop), too
often the pain of experiencing oppression or bearing witness to it is reduced in
a public claim that "all lives matter." Or as we summarize the constant barrage
of oppression we experience, we are told it is simply a "personal" experience
(at best), a personal character flaw (at worse). And through the gaze of others,
these oppressions are all too often characterized as something small, insignificant, or unimportant.

Here, I want to try to reflexively magnify the ways and means that Black
women's lives matter. I want to (re)member the stories created and lived by
Black women everywhere, to make visible the nature of this (re)membering
and the ways that we declare our right to survival and existence as Black
women who also lead. I'm suggesting that to truly appreciate the complexities of who we are and why we matter, people of color and people of spiritual
consciousness must **both** engage with Black cultural knowledge and wisdom,
the goal being to develop and truly being able to *see* Black women as *Black*
women. Appiah (1992) calls this a task of learning to read *productively*. He further suggests that productive reading must engage the *collective* and complex
history of Black peoples as we create homeplace wherever we are in the world.

I want to tell a story of the ways this collective and complex history shows
up in the ways Black women love, even as we often suffer in "a society full of
institutionalized and violent hatred for both [our dark] skins and [our] female
bodies" (Bethel, 1982, p. 178). I want to share the ways we feel besieged,
experience our lives, and make a way through both on behalf of our humanity
and in honor of the countless others on whose shoulders we stand. These
are the ancestors whom Julie Dash describes as those "who *chose* to survive"
(Dash, 1991). For those of us in education who wish to center our work in
spaces that embody *and* produce diversity, equity, and justice, our explorations
must move to a place where we can see, hear, and recognize the depth of the
voices heard in the recent rallying cry of our young people: *Black lives matter*.
The central argument here is an echo of their words: That the declarations of
love and sovereignty that Black women make, as we suffer under the weight

of racism and sexism, can expand our collective understanding of *how* all lives matter.

The following is a narrative written in 1995 while I was serving as an assistant dean for equity and diversity at a large, predominantly White research 1 institution. As might be imagined, the work of being an assistant dean was often carried out in contexts and spaces of resistance and opposition, both passive and aggressive. At its best, it was also carried out in spaces and contexts that embodied pure joy, spaces where the goals of equity, justice, and respect for our multiple humanity and diversity was affirmed. This narrative was written in the form of a memo, one that I "wished" I could've shared without severe repercussions, as an early career faculty member. It was also crafted in response to a number of derogatory comments from a colleague about the need (or perceived lack of need) to develop programs, dialogues, and systems of support for students of color as they pursued degrees in the predominantly White university where I worked. I share this story here so that the reader might understand the often silent sufferings of Black women who serve and lead, so that you might hear the quiet sufferings that are the racialized realities and experiences as we live them, the ways that we are perceived, heard, and sometimes (mis)understood by White colleagues who dismiss racism and racial violence as not really harmful, as an inherent part of our DNA versus as systemic, structural, and cultural erasures and exclusions that cause harm and injury to Blacks and other people of color. The unfortunate part about the following memo? Serving in the role as a department chair now, over 20 years later, my memo would read much the same.

Sometimes It's Hard to Do This Work: Being Black Women and Leading with Our Lives[1].

<u>MEMO</u>

TO: Those who want to know at least part of the reason why Black women leaders might have an attitude in the academy

FROM: Cynthia B. Dillard

RE: My daily life as an Assistant Dean who is also a Black woman

DATE: April 1995 (Revised in 2016)

I am looking for real colleagues.

I am looking for real, honest colleagues.

Not folks who assume from jump street that I've arrived in the Dean's office or the academy solely because of affirmative action, but folks who don't think that my leadership and teaching, particularly at a "prestigious" university, requires an extraordinary explanation for my being there.

I am looking for real honest colleagues who assume that my ways of being (my culture), my ways of knowing (my theory), and my ways of leading (culturally engaged) are not any less rigorous or righteous or real than their own but instead a place from which I center and make sense of my

---

work as an African American woman. These real colleagues do not see a conflict between theory and cultural/experiential explanations as principles which guide thought and action, but recognize that it is that sort of didactical framing that inherently continues to advance a traditionally racist and sexist agenda, particularly in leadership and educational research.

In other words, I am looking for colleagues who do not believe that the bell curve really exists.

I am looking for real honest colleagues. Colleagues who are comfortable enough with their own constructions of their own humanity to respect mine. Who aren't scared of talking about the ways that racism, or classism, or sexism, or homophobia shape our decisions about policies and programs within education. Folks who know that those are the very conversations that will breathe life into an academy that thrives on reproducing privilege and inequality at every turn.

I am looking for good honest colleagues who will not ask the question: "what is it like to be a Black woman administrator? Oh yea, I've got about five minutes," but instead will, over a glass of wine, cup of coffee, or a meal (and as a *regular* ongoing part of their lives), engage in the *reciprocal* dialogues and struggles necessary to actually hear my response—the blood, sweat, and tears, as well as the joy, the sensuality, the hopefulness, the spirit-filled nature of my being in and choosing administration as part of my academic life.

I am looking for colleagues who will understand why many Black women do not separate our "academic" work from the rest of our life's work, from advocacy work on behalf and in the very communities of color and women who nurture us, who take us in, who patch us up after what feels like a lifetime of struggle to survive the often brutal realities of the professoriate. We are intimately connected to our communities and must give homage to those whose work it has been to sit with us, talk with us, feed us, bandage us up, hug us, and remind us of the legacy of strong women and men of color who have come before us. It is only then, after we have been pushed back to strength, that our communities of care send us away from these homeplaces, better and stronger advocates for the struggle of opportunity and human rights, especially in educational contexts.

I am looking for colleagues who can see that there are deep connections between being Black women leaders, mothers, lovers, teachers and scholars that informs our work. These colleagues must recognize too that inherent in being one of the too few sisters who have successfully navigated a way through the maze of higher education leadership, I have a higher moral responsibility that transcends being widely published in the top journals, beyond being "politically correct." In other words, women leaders of color and consciousness, while fully cognizant of and attentive to the requirements of tenure, promotion, and a scholarly life must also pay attention in our research, teaching, and leadership to Alice Walker's (1983) call for "each one to pull one [or more]."

In this vein, I am particularly looking for some leadership colleagues who say out loud that they "don't believe [I'm] ready for a promotion to full-time Associate Dean" but two months later, after learning that I am a finalist for a Deanship at a prestigious private university suddenly discover my enormous talent and value to the institution. "An associate deanship is yours if you'd like it ..."

Yea, I am looking for some real honest colleagues.

I am yearning for some honest colleagues who know there is no such thing as an acceptable joke about race or gender or sexual orientation/affiliation and other honest colleagues who will "go off" without my being there;

I am seeking some I-am-equally-responsible-for-engaging-and-dialoging-in-the-most-honest-ways-I-can kinds of colleagues;

I am looking for, searching for and in some cases am fortunate enough to have found honest colleagues who are not intimidated or confused by the power and magic of women of color who choose to be leaders. Especially articulate, bright, well-published, award winning, successful, gorgeous, connected, righteous Black women intellectual leaders who do not want to be rendered invisible in order to be accepted or acceptable in higher education. Do you know any colleagues like that?

Theorizing Suffering, Marshaling Strength and Love

According to Armah (2002), Black people are thinkers and sharers. But we think, he states, in *order* to share. As I re-read the above narrative and have read and heard so many similar narratives from Black women leaders over the years, I realize even more deeply that my existence—and that of all Black women—is built on the legacy of people who declared their *sovereign right to life* in a state of hate. And to be clear: Choosing to act when one's humanity and brilliance are denied and to stand instead in your truth does have consequences. And in that way, I am simply in awe of Black people. I am in awe of our resilience and strength, in awe of the ways, we have *chosen* life and love even with so much hatred as the backdrop. Lightfoot (1994) says this:

> You know where the minefields are ... there is wisdom ... You are in touch with the ancestors ... and it is from the gut, not rationally figured out. Black women have to use this all the time, of course, the creativity is still there, but we are not fools ... we call it the "epistemological privileges of the oppressed." How do you tap that wisdom—name it, mine it, pass it on to the next generation? (p. 59)

The story shared here provides just a glimpse of the complexity of living life in a context of racism and sexism and the dignity of our declarations of love as Black women. The intention here is not to present Black women victimized, unable, or unwilling to recognize even our own complicity at times, especially when we resist or are not willing to talk back within the racist, sexist, and homophobic institutions where we work. It is further not the intention to present ourselves and our lives as "always acting from the position of powerlessness that white supremacy defines as our place" (hooks, 1995, p. 269). There is instead, a strong historical ethos of commitment to our lives in honor of spaces of affinity and support, namely our families, communities, and ancestors. It also represents a commitment to an endarkened feminist stance, a stance that embodies the love so central to our very breath. Embodied within these voices are specialized knowledges that theorize a dismantling standpoint of and for African American women and that encompass a coherent and dynamic epistemology. It is a place from which to theorize the realities of Black women through situating our knowledge and actions in the cultural spaces out of which they arose.

We lead and love as Black women in a place that has never affirmed Black womanhood. *So we affirm it for ourselves.* And in our affirmations are several bold and important lessons understood and lived by Black women yesterday, today, and tomorrow.

When we speak of suffering and strength, Collins (2000) guides us, arguing that Black women, out of necessity, have relied on a collective set of experiences particular to Black women and from which our worldview arises. Other scholars in adult education such as Sheared (1994) and Johnson-Bailey (2001) have discussed this as well. Given racism that pervades the social fabric of Black life in the diaspora, Black women have had access to and created a different epistemology by which we assess truth, one that is widely accepted within our communities. As Black women, an understanding of the distinction between knowledge and wisdom is crucial to our survival: We "cannot afford to be fools of any type, for our objectification as other denies us the protections that White skin, maleness, and wealth confer" (Collins, 2000, p. 257). So, drawing on earlier work, I want to speak to three lessons of wisdom we might learn from standing next to the wounds of Black women's lives (heard in the earlier narrative) that "when shared and passed on, become the collective wisdom of Black women's experiences" (Collins, 2000, p. 256). Said another way, what can we learn from the wisdom of Black women's suffering in contexts of race, racism, sexism, and the violence of all and how might we address the violence of these oppressions?

First, *engaging in deep and sustained dialogue with Black women leaders is key to understanding our realities, experiences, culture, and leadership—and to inform your own as well.* I often describe our stories about identity and personhood as gifts. So if we understand that what Black women leaders are doing—and what meaning we are making of what we are doing—then we will understand that when we offer a glimpse into our pain, dreams, hopes, whatever, it might be received with open hands: Gently and honorably, treasured for the gift that it is. Otherwise, Black women risk continued silence for the sake of self-preservation and those around us do not receive the benefit of

New Directions for Adult and Continuing Education • DOI: 10.1002/ace

the legacy of wisdom and brilliance that we are. Audre Lorde's (1984) words serve to en-courage Black women to speak as an act of decolonization of our spirits, minds, and bodies, regardless of the attempts by others to silence us when she bravely says: "I was going to die, if not sooner then later, whether or not I had ever spoken myself. My silences had not protected me. Your silences will not protect you either" (p. 41). She goes on to call on the legacy of generations of Black women that can be accounted for when any one of us speaks:

> But for every real word spoken, for every attempt I ever made to speak those truths for which I am still seeking . . . it was the concern and caring of all those women which gave me strength and enabled me to scrutinize the essentials of my living. (p. 41)

The challenge Black women face is to choose be in dialogue even through our anger, even in the face of the contemporary assaults of structural, social, and personal racism. This is full of risks in cross-racial/gender dialogues. And the challenge for those who are not Black is to *choose to stay in these dialogues with us*. In the midst of the anger and disappointment, we can then *both* (re)member (that is recall *and* put back together again) the pain and realizations that, from a spiritual lens, show us that our heritages are mutually constituted (Dillard, 2012; Dillard & Okpalaoka, 2011). As Black and other women and men engage in such dialogues, we all have to learn to speak words in ways that have love at the center, especially love of ourselves. And the dialogue for Blacks is about laying down the burden of racism and sexism and other injuries in order to heal. And this healing is done to also heal someone else who has suffered. But we realize that in order to do the work of leadership, we must show up strong and whole, with a great sense of what work is ours to do, our purpose for being here at this moment on this earth as Black women. Again Audre Lorde's (1984) words are key here:

> My fullest concentration of energy is available to me only when I integrate all the parts of who I am, openly . . . Only then can I bring myself and my energies as a whole to the service of those struggles which I embrace as part of my living. (pp. 120–121)

That brings us to the second lesson: That healing of one's whole self is critical to doing race and identity work and comes from learning to listen with the body, mind, *and* spirit, not privileging minds or personalities. As mentioned in the narrative, our healing as Black women arises from choices we make. Despite the anger. Despite the pain. Despite our weariness at folks continuing to expect us to always teach them about race, nationality, gender, or difference. Despite the ignorant questions and assumptions about us, bell hooks (1992) says:

I choose to create in my daily life/ spaces of reconciliation and forgiveness/
Where I let go of past hurt, fear and shame/ And hold each other close/
It is only in the act and practice/Of loving Blackness/That we are able
to reach and embrace the world/ Without destructive bitterness/And ongoing
collective rage. (p. 1)

My experiences suggest that part of our healing is wrapped up in being
honest and focused, in dogged pursuit of our work *as* Black women. Such response is possible when we are spiritually grounded, both individually as well
as in a cultural community. And, as the brilliant Dr. Chinwe Okpalaoka states:
"If everyone involved in a relationship is in it for the long haul, then it is critical to work through the necessary 'mess' and believe that, because of love and
spirit, we will be okay on the other side" (Okpalaoka & Dillard, 2011, p. 70).
This is *very* intimate talk, where one must raise questions not just to the other,
but maybe more importantly to the self. These inner spaces have been sometimes painful and difficult spaces to explore across race. Many Black women
have described what we've come to call psychic assaults, places where we have
been both disconnected from or distorted through our roots/heritages. Further,
these may also be places where we ourselves have purposely disconnected or
distorted ourselves in order to survive psychic assaults. But deep cross-racial
dialogue can happen only if we build relationships of trust first. This is the final
lesson to address suffering of Black women leaders: *Build trusting relationships
first.* Appiah (1992) talks about the need to understand and know another
deeply and culturally as a prerequisite to a productive reading of one another's
lived experiences. This is the way we might address the wounds of another.
However, every person's understandings of personhood—of who we are and
how we "be"—are grounded in our own cultural realities. Thus, we come to
race talk *differently*, with varying experiences of race, racism, sexism, classism,
homophobia, even as they are aspects of our collective humanity. We often
have really different experiences of the ways that culture and race work in the
world (historically, structurally, and spiritually). So there's the need to listen
deeply and it's difficult to balance those differences with talk about/through
race, as it raises imbalance in positioning, as we've known it, particularly in
leadership. Who is center? Who is marginalized? Shifting positionalities can
open possibilities to build deep relationships if the conversation can (a) remain *on the wounds inflicted and the injury of racism, sexism, etc*, and (b) does
not dismiss realities and experiences that we may not have personally had that
may be unknown to us. So for Black women who often have lifetimes of experiences with race and racism, there is the weight of that experience. What
do we do with it? Marshaling discourses of spirituality that heal something
bigger than ourselves seems the sort of liberatory healing that was called for
in the earlier narrative: Of the need to literally set the burden and weight of
experiences of racism and sexism down in order to heal myself and so that
others can also heal. And to be clear: I am not arguing here for forgetfulness:
I am arguing here for a (re)membering of such oppressions as a way toward

healing, toward developing mutual trust. So the larger lesson rests in bearing witness to the struggles of Black women—leaders and otherwise—as we articulate and sooth the injuries of racism and sexism with a balm of love generally and of loving Blackness particularly. This is the counter-narrative. Like hooks (2000) suggests, such love includes trust, empathy, respect, forgiveness, compassion, honesty, sincerity, joy, etc. Most important, such love is a move away from fear and holding back and toward leaning in, toward an embrace of the emotionality and vulnerability of our unknowns together. Let it be so.

Note

1. This narrative is a slightly revised excerpt from an earlier publication by the author: Dillard, C. B. (2000). The substance of things hoped for, the evidence of things not seen: Examining an endarkened feminist epistemology in educational research and leadership. *International Journal of Qualitative Studies in Education, 13*(6), 661–681.

References

Appiah, A. (1992). *In my father's house: Africa in the philosophy of culture*. New York, NY: Oxford University Press.

Armah, A. K. (2002). *KMT: In the house of life: An epistemic novel*. Popenguine, Senegal: Per Ankh.

Bethel, L. (1982). "This infinity of conscious pain": Zora Neale Hurston and the Black female literary tradition. In G. T. Hull, P. B. Scott, & B. Smith (Eds.), *All the women are white, all the Blacks are men, but some of us are brave* (pp. 176–188). New York, NY: Feminist Press.

Collins, P. H. (2000). *Black feminist thought: Knowledge, consciousness, and the politics of empowerment*. New York, NY: Routledge.

Dash, J. (Producer/Director). (1991). *Daughters of the dust* [Motion picture]. United States: Geechee Girls Productions.

Dillard, C. B. (2006). *On spiritual strivings: Transforming an African American woman's academic life*. Albany, NY: State University of New York Press.

Dillard, C. B. (2012). *Learning to (re)member the things we've learned to forget: Endarkened feminisms, spirituality and the sacred nature of research*. New York, NY: Peter Lang.

Dillard, C. B., & Okpalaoka, C. L. (2011). The sacred and spiritual nature of endarkened transnational feminist praxis in qualitative research. In N. K. Denzin & Y. S. Lincoln (Eds.), *The Sage handbook of qualitative research* (4th ed., pp. 147–162). Los Angeles, CA: Sage.

hooks, b. (1992). *Black looks: Race and representation*. Boston, MA: South End Press.

hooks, b. (1995). Feminism in black and white. In M. Golden & S. R. Shreve (Eds.), *Skin deep: Black women and white women write about race* (pp. 265–277). New York, NY: Doubleday.

hooks, b. (2000). *All about love: New visions*. New York, NY: William Morrow and Company.

Johnson-Bailey, J. (2001). *Sistahs in college: Making a way out of no way*. Malabar, FL: Krieger Press.

Lightfoot, S. L. (1994). *I've known rivers: Lives of loss and liberation*. Reading, MA: Addison-Wesley.

Lorde, A. (1984). *Sister outsider*. Freedom, CA: The Crossing Press.

Okpalaoka, C. L., & Dillard, C. B. (2011). Our healing is next to the wound: Endarkened feminisms, spirituality, and wisdom for teaching, learning and research. In E. J. Tisdell & A. L. Swarz (Eds.), *New Directions for Adult and Continuing Education: No. 131. Adult education and the pursuit of wisdom* (pp. 65–74). San Francisco, CA: Jossey-Bass.

Peck, M. S. (1978). *The road less traveled: A new psychology of love, traditional values and spiritual growth.* New York, NY: Touchtone.

Sheared, V. (1994). Giving voice: An inclusive model of instruction—A womanist perspective. In E. Hayes & S. A. J. Colin III. (Eds.), *New Directions for Adult and Continuing Education: No. 61. Confronting racism and sexism* (pp. 27–37). San Francisco, CA: Jossey-Bass.

Walker, A. (1983). *In search of our mother's gardens: Womanist prose.* San Diego, CA: Harcourt Brace Jovanovich.

CYNTHIA B. DILLARD, PhD (Nana Mansa II of Mpeasem, Ghana, West Africa), is Mary Frances Early Professor of Teacher Education and Department Chair; Director, Ghana Study Abroad in Education Program; Department of Educational Theory and Practice, The University of Georgia.

New Directions for Adult and Continuing Education • DOI: 10.1002/ace

4

In this chapter, the authors decenter soulless curricular and administrative practices in collegiate settings and re-conceptualize justice work through faith as a labor of love.

Womanist Pedagogical Love as Justice Work on College Campuses: Reflections from Faithful Black Women Academics

Kirsten T. Edwards, Valerie J. Thompson

[The Lord] has shown you, O [wo]man, what is good. And what does the LORD require of you? To act justly and to love mercy and to walk humbly with your GOD.

Micah 6:8 New International Version [NIV]

Reflection

Much of higher education literature is beginning to explore the need for diversity on college campuses. Moving beyond exposure and tolerance, many scholars have theorized the role of higher education in the development of allies; individuals who not only recognize systemic injustice, but commit themselves to the co-conspiratorial work of dismantling institutionalized hegemony in community with the oppressed.

Within the ally development literature, there is a troubling theme. Overprivileged individuals often struggle to productively collaborate with minoritized communities (Munin & Speight, 2010; Reason & Broido, 2005). The phenomenon also manifests within minoritized communities, as movements trouble the intersections of systemic oppression (Crenshaw, 1991; Edwards, 2014). Although their intentions may be righteous, due to the power of systemic oppression, their actions are often laced with the character of domination (Freire, 1968/2007). Because of their more enfranchised situatedness, overprivileged justice workers are often less likely/willing to interrogate themselves at the level necessary to enact meaningful resistance. Minoritized communities lament the expectation on the part of allies to be praised and rewarded by their less enfranchised peers. Sadly, allies often fail to realize that

New Directions for Adult and Continuing Education, no. 152, Winter 2016 © 2016 Wiley Periodicals, Inc.
Published online in Wiley Online Library (wileyonlinelibrary.com) • DOI: 10.1002/ace.20211

the work of liberation is for their own salvation and not a sacrificial offering *given* to the oppressed (Freire, 1968/2007; hooks, 2004).

Searching for a Better Way

In many ways, critiques of allies and ally development are essentially evaluations of justice work that center the ego-self. They are challenges that emerge when those who are socialized to occupy the center assume that righteousness can materialize as an act of their independent will. This approach is antithetical to justice work at multiple levels. First, it participates in the Western notion of the (imperialist) "individual" and predicates the pursuit of justice on the disposition of the autonomous self, a presumed fixed and unconnected being who has ultimate power over *his* surroundings, the *Master* of his universe. Second, it assumes that this (overprivileged) self is naturally endowed with the necessary insight to effectively interrogate the ubiquity of intersecting systems of oppression and insert *himself* into the work of dismantling that which *he* has un/consciously but/and self-servingly built. These are both notions rooted in Western conceptions of reason, logic, and rationality that exalt the mind as separate from and above the body and spirit.

We suggest in this essay that as religiospiritual Black Christian women (Arnold, 2014; Edwards, 2015), rooted in the U.S. Black Church tradition, we bring insights to justice work that disrupt both of these propositions. Our aim is not to position ourselves as occupying some pure space of objectivity, free from bias. Nor are we attempting to exalt ourselves as models of character and goodness. Instead, we assert our subjectivity *in the Spirit* and *at the margins* of adult and higher education and the insight that marginal positionality provides to interrogate justice work (Lorde, 2008; Tisdell, 2003).

Drawing on womanist theology as well as other spiritually Black and feminized frames, this essay attempts to reframe resistance as not primarily an intellectual project that exalts the rational thinking *man*, but instead a spiritual practice (Dillard, 2012). As a scholar (Kirsten) and a practitioner (Valerie), together we explore the multidimensionality of the Spirit in collegiate settings. In both regards, we deliberately decenter the sterile (soulless) curricular and administrative practices that are bound by Eurocentrist notions of logic and rationality that glorify the presumption of an *omnipotent self* (Baszile, 2008). By doing so, the present treatise reconceptualizes justice work on college campuses as *love labor* that can be informed by the communal knowledges and workings of faithful Black women.

Differences: Womanism, Feminism, and Black Resistance

> Those of us who stand outside the circle of this society's definition of acceptable women; those of us who have been forged in the crucibles of difference—those of us who are poor, who are lesbians, who are Black, who are older—know that

survival is not an academic skill. It is learning how to take our differences and make them strengths. For the master's tools will never dismantle the master's house. (Lorde, 2008, p. 50)

The seemingly prophetic words of Audre Lorde harken to Black women's role as not only an oppressed class but also leaders in the production of a more just society. Like Jesus and the biblical saints, our pain must serve a purpose. We are *called* to root our activism in our experiences of oppression and denial. As *Hagar's Daughters*, the rejection and abandonment we have endured at the hands of patriarchy, racism, and classism (Hayes, 1995) open the door for God's promise of a new nation—a new model of academic equity and access—to be revealed.

We are also particularly cognizant of the impotent pursuit of accessing contaminated fruit. Unlike our Black brothers and white sisters, we are acutely aware that the spoiled manna of patriarchy and white supremacy will not give us the nourishment necessary for the journey to the Promised Land. Black women resistors operating from a religiospiritual frame are uniquely positioned to recognize the milk and honey of social justice.

In *White Women's Christ and Black Women's Jesus* Grant (1989), while articulating the value of women's experience, challenges the field of religious studies with the following question: "The struggle of women in the church is not only one of the political process of ordination or leadership, but it involves, as we shall see, theological issues, such as, are women human and can women represent Christ?" (p. 9). Migrating Grant's question to the broader postsecondary context, we ask: "The struggle of *Black* women in the *Academy* is not only one of the political process of *matriculation and professional advancement*, but it involves, as we shall see, *ethical and moral issues*, such as, are *Black* women human and can *Black* women represent the *Academy*?" And if Black women do not represent the Academy, what do their experiences *reflect about* the Academy? If we are relegated to a perpetual "outsider within" status (Collins, 1990), what does our condition say about the moral health of postsecondary education and possibly its need for a spiritually reflective turn? Making honest assessments about our condition, we recognize faithful practice as a necessary response to the circumstances of academic life, as opposed to an individualized solution or cultural relic. Deep reflection on our experiences as religiospiritual Black women confirms to us the illness in the soul of higher education, and the balm necessary for healing.

A Little Housekeeping

This section problematizes metaphors that stereotype Black women in their roles in academe. Metaphors serve to devalue Black women as intellectuals and cast them in the image of institutional housekeepers.

Black Women as Maids of Academe. In some ways, the differences in faithful Black women's academic experiences are evidentiary of their

New Directions for Adult and Continuing Education • DOI: 10.1002/ace

status of living at the intersections of multiple oppressions. Black women are often hired as representations of color and gender with unstated expectations of work overload, which include commitments to committees and countless minoritized student populations (Gregory, 1999; Harley, 2008). At the root of these experiences are issues of racism, sexism, feelings of isolation, and campus climate. On the road to success, Black women are also subjected to unwritten rules and expectations related to the focus and quantity of their work, as well as their service to the institution. These pressures often create a climate of exclusion and invalidation.

Black women's experiences in the academy are not unlike their experiences in the church. As Grant (1982) states,

> It is often said that women are the "backbone" of the church ... It has become apparent to me that most of the ministers who use this term are referring to location rather than function. What they really mean is that women are in the background and should be kept there: they are merely support workers. (p. 141)

In this way, the Black Church becomes an interesting frame from which to analyze the labor of faithful academic Black women. A religious organizational analysis is even more applicable when one considers the role of faith, specifically the Christian faith, in the success and endurance of Black women in the academy (Cozart, 2010; Watt, 2003). At all levels, from undergraduate study to professional appointment, religiospiritual faith practices and beliefs have emerged as a consistently positive influence on the academic experiences of Black women in the United States. Religiospirituality acts as a protective barrier from the violence of the academy.

Nevertheless, when this theme of faith and perseverance is assessed through the prism of the Black Church, an interesting dichotomy surfaces. As is the case within faith communities, Black women have historically and consistently contributed powerful support and direction to colleges and universities. And like their church sisters, their efforts have gone largely unacknowledged. Much of their labor that has pushed both the Black Church and the white academy toward more substantive practices to meet the needs of the "least of these" has come at the cost of their subordination and *unvisibility* (McKittrick, 2006). These challenges manifest in particular ways for students, faculty, and practitioners.

Black Women as Love Laborers. With all of the evidence considered, it would suggest that religiospiritual Black women are, as Harley (2008) writes, "maids [in] academe." We are the silen(ced)t intellectual and administrative domestic workers. However, as we argue, by reframing our work in the institution through a spiritual lens as resistant agential love labor, we are better able to see the potent effects of our subjectivities. Like our Black Church foremothers, who loved and labored within a patriarchal and misogynistic religious community that consigned Black women to roles as choir members, children's Sunday school teachers, and church secretaries, we continue to locate the

New Directions for Adult and Continuing Education • DOI: 10.1002/ace

necessary "interpretive space" (Coulter & Smith, 2009, p. 577) to subversively resist for the betterment of the whole community (Higginbotham, 1993).

Conceptual Roots: Womanist Theology

As mentioned previously, in an effort to better explore the potential for Black feminized spiritual practice in academic work, we draw on womanist theology (Grant, 1989; Hayes, 1995). Womanist theology emerges as a faithful response to Alice Walker's (1983) womanism. Firmly rooted in the Black liberation theological tradition, womanist theologians take up issues of faith, religious practice, scholarship, resistance, justice, and Black womanhood in an integrative manner. As a theoretical tradition, womanist theology meaningfully explores the intersectional relationship between faith and reason within a Black feminized context, not as contradictory but instead complementary and interdependent.

Not only is womanist theology a spiritual turn in womanism, but it also has at its core resistance, as womanist theology was forged in the context of silence in the field of religious studies (Cannon, 1995). Black women theologians found themselves written out of not only Black Church studies but also feminist religious studies (Cannon, 1995; Grant, 1989). These ongoing exclusions prepared early womanist theologians with the aptitudes and proficiencies necessary to build bridges across difference for survival and extended love practice. Their work and theorizing provide some of the earliest modern models of love-centered allyship; approaches that also emerge from the standpoint (Collins, 1990) of marginalization and erasure.

Methodological Deliverance: Scholarly Rearing

The present project draws on an emerging methodological frame: "Scholarly Rearing" (Edwards & Baszile, 2016). Edwards and Baszile describe scholarly rearing as:

> Black women['s] textual labor of writing ourselves in as acts of individual and collective resistance. [Scholarly rearing also] shift[s] attention from the power the writer experiences through testifying to the development the student [or reader] experiences through reading ... Textual pedagogy refers to the ways in which Black women writers and readers evoke the art of teaching and learning. These pedagogical moments are serendipitous, invocative, faith-filled, and spiritual ... by virtue of their truth-telling in writing [and narrating], which is often an act of faith and spirit, they create the epistemic space where they can teach what is often silenced. (Edwards & Baszile, 2016, p. 87)

This spirit-filled methodology centers the development of the next generation of Black women academicians. It also foregrounds relationship in academic practice. Scholarly rearing challenges researchers to place less emphasis on speaking to a disciplinary audience—one that is disinclined to appreciate a Black feminized spiritual perspective—and more concerned with the survival of the oppressed. It shifts the researcher's priorities and purpose by highlighting traditional methodological frames' allegiance to epistemic erasure. Moreover, by supporting culturally specific theorizing and practice, scholarly rearing gives the next generation of Black women scholars permission to live and think authentically.

Scholarly rearing draws from three traditions: womanist theology, Black liberation theology specifically Black Church testimony (Lincoln & Mamiya, 1990), and indigenous methodologies (Ng-A-Fook, 2007). Looking *toward* our foremothers' creative resistant inventions, such as old Negro spirituals, the rhythms and prose we produce in our academic enslavement not only encourage our spirits, but they also have carefully coded within them the map to freedom for our community. By enacting scholarly rearing, we evoke the longstanding practice of Black academic women to provide guidance and deliverance through our testimonies.

What follows are our individual but interconnected testimonies. As we narrate our lives in the academy, we invite the reader to identify the embedded messages of faith and love. The cornerstone of scholarly rearing is to gather hope and strength in the midst of what may be a painful recounting. In this way, oppression doesn't end at the point of trauma, but instead is deployed for loving and emancipatory purposes.

Kirsten's Testimony.   Over the years, I have developed a pretty consistent pre- and postteaching routine. Five to 10 minutes before class begins, I usually sit in my office and pray quietly. I invite the Holy Spirit to meet my students and me in the classroom. I ask the Lord to give me wisdom and direction. I pray that the class will be intellectually rewarding and that we will all walk away more committed to justice in higher education. But most significantly, I ask the Lord to remove all fear and anxiety from my heart, to give me boldness mixed with love.

The battle with fear and anxiety has become a hallmark of my professorial life. Even now, I am breathing through and fighting against the tightness in my chest and sinking in the pit of my stomach, which have become my constant companions when writing. This evil overseer waits for me to wake in the mornings, takes a seat at my writing table, and taunts me as I struggle to bring together prose and frame into a coherent idea. Fear and anxiety don't just accompany my writing time and teaching. I feel these unholy siblings while engaging colleagues, preparing for tenure and promotion, presenting at conferences, as well as other "scholarly" activities. They are ever present.

It would be easy to suggest that all I need is a better self-perception, more confidence, stronger networking skills. But all of those solutions would ignore the veracity of the "interlocking systems of oppression" (Collins, 1990, p. 3) weighing on my life and work. The fear and anxiety I experience are the result of an unjust relationship bequeathed to me by virtue of being born Black and female. As I peel back the layers of analysis, I hear the voice of God:

New Directions for Adult and Continuing Education • DOI: 10.1002/ace

There is no fear in love. But perfect love drives out fear, because fear has to do with punishment. The one who fears is not made perfect in love. 1 John 4:18 [NIV]

The preceding scripture becomes most relevant when I consider the complexity of my life as a minoritized scholar. I'm not simply struggling against insecurities and diminished self-perception. Fear and anxiety are in many respects a natural result of the oppressive context in which I labor. It emerges in relationship with systemic domination. Therefore, my recovery must attend to this relationship. My pursuit after God-love not only ministers to my self-reflection, but it also frees me from conceding to oppression's power. *Because fear has to do with punishment,* God-love leads me out of the punisher/oppressor-punished/oppressed frame and into a reflection on my divine purpose, the good plan God has for my life that supersedes the oppressive academic system.

"For I know the plans I have for you," declares the Lord, "plans to prosper you and not to harm you, plans to give you hope and a future." Jeremiah 29:11 [NIV].

As I've become more spiritually cognizant of my professional purpose, I've begun to realize that fear and anxiety are not only natural manifestations of stressful work. They are also spiritual attacks on my divine purpose. As a Christian, I am called to infuse love into every aspect of my life. As a faithful Black woman steeped in the Black/womanist theological tradition, I am compelled to deploy love as a revolutionary practice (Cannon, 1995; Grant, 1989). My responsibility to love and be loved as justice work requires disciplined practice. It requires a daily/hourly/moment-by-moment reorientation to the world and the academy. Particular scriptures have become my reframing tools. I command myself regularly:

Do not be anxious about anything, but in every situation, by prayer and petition, with thanksgiving, present your requests to God. And the peace of God, which transcends all understanding, will guard your hearts and your minds in Christ Jesus. Philippians 4:6–7 [NIV]

As a spiritually disciplined practice of resistance, I have learned to speak peace *into* my soul. I have learned to "call those things that are not as though they were" (Romans 4:17 King James Version [KJV]). I work to recognize the "unrealness" of the academy's illogical "objectivity" and commitment to Eurocentric rationality that undermines Africentric-feminized ways of knowing and being in the world. These spiritual tools help me see again the preeminence of the spiritual world; a world in which Black women are created, commissioned, and loved by a holy God.

Valerie's Testimony. I opened my eyes, took a deep breath, and prayed that I would be able to face my reality. I understood that every moment that the Lord allowed me to see was a blessing. However, I found myself dreading my existence. The person who I was 6 months ago would not have recognized the woman I had become. Daily I was told how I was not the ideal choice for the position and how others would have been more preferable. No matter how early I arrived or how late I stayed, nothing was ever good enough for the toxic oppressor who was my supervisor. The headaches came almost immediately, followed by an extreme fatigue that remained regardless of how much sleep I had gotten. Although I was a woman of faith, daily cuts that triggered and targeted my personhood left me too emotionally exhausted to start the day fighting yet again. I was experiencing the first level of burnout and I truly needed a reprieve ...

I was unable to pinpoint the exact intersection of my injuries; I just knew that they ached more every day, and that they were having a drastic effect on my self-identified calling. This perspective was much deeper than a vocation. This *call* was woven into the intricacies of my identities as a Black, Christian, and woman within higher education. Unfortunately, due to the dysfunction that was my reality, the concept of workplace burnout became my truth and my call felt like a distant memory.

Working While Burning. The concept of workplace burnout is not one that was originally used within the field of higher education. Although there are many definitions of burnout, the most widely used definition is a psychological syndrome of emotional exhaustion, depersonalization, and reduced personal accomplishment in response to chronic interpersonal stressors on the job (Maslach, Schaufeli, & Leiter, 2001). Through the lens of this definition, the three key dimensions of this phenomenon are an overwhelming exhaustion, feelings of cynicism and detachment from the job, and sense of ineffectiveness and lack of accomplishment.

Faith in Action: The Embers of Burning. Although multiple studies have identified several identity groups that are at high risk for burnout such as women, introverts, and young professionals in student affairs (Howard-Hamilton Palmer, Johnson, & Kicklighter, 1998), theorizing burnout through the intersectional lens of a faithful Black woman presents a unique opportunity. It allows me to investigate the ways in which faith has been used as a "healing balm" (Miller, 2003, p. 307) that treated me for the painful burns caused by my professional space. It illuminated a way to appropriately view faith in action in times of excessive stress and strain. However, just saying a prayer or a scripture was not enough to receive healing. As stated in Luke 5:4, it required a decisive action that challenged me to launch out into the deep to activate it. Before I could launch out, I had to first understand that burnout is directly antithetical to how I should see myself and my challenges as a faithful Black woman.

Within our spiritual toolbox as Black women of faith, we are equipped with biblical weapons that prepare us for any impending battles that we may

New Directions for Adult and Continuing Education • DOI: 10.1002/ace

encounter. Those weapons do not, however, excuse us from the battle. Rather, they prepare us for the journey. Spirituality, faith, and religiosity are not terms that can be used without action; they must be applied with the intentional decision to move. For me, it was more than the black and red writings that held inspirational passages wrapping me in the loving embrace of my heavenly Father. I needed to take those passages and do what they commanded me to do in the academy. It was time to abandon "faith without works" (James 2:14 KJV).

The first decision to *work* my faith came as a result of the directive I was given in Matthew 5:44 NIV to begin to "pray for those who persecute" me. This I must admit was no easy task. The daily microaggressions I experienced made it almost impossible to think of any good words for my oppressors. Still I prayed. Although the prayer was not long, I earnestly prayed for my enemy. Although my oppressors had harmed me, they were only a portion of a grander plan. It was not about them as oppressor as much as it was about me as the believer. My second chance came in the form of a tiny bottle filled with blessing oil. The fragrant oil's smell immediately alerts anyone who has woken up as a child with it on their forehead. The oil served as an act of defiance against how I had been treated. With every oily mark I left on the doors, chairs, and walls, I gained a spiritual confidence that enabled me to see the situation not for what it appeared to be in the natural but for what it could be in faith. The most powerful tool of resistance I wielded was the words that I spoke demanding the atmosphere to come into alignment with my faith. The revolution that was my faith in action became the way that I survived.

Benediction: Reflections and Concluding Thoughts

What our testimonies suggest is that we, as faithful Black women academics, enact deliberately religiospiritual resistance. We recite scriptures that affirm our value and power in an institutional context that consistently devalues and disempowers us. We sanctify and anoint with oil as an act of claiming and re-redefining physical space, while actively receiving messages that we do not belong. We pray over impending meetings, class sessions, and colleagues, believing that God will meet us there and protect our personhood while giving us successful interactions. We do this within an institutional framework which insists that our only recourse is bureaucratic, knowing full- well that Black women are regularly not vindicated in these judicial proceedings.

Decolonizing the Spirit: Acts and Artifacts of Resistance. All of these faithful, contradictory acts become for us Womanist Decolonizing Practice. We are decolonizing the secularizing of our lives and spirits. Our practices center the power of love and the spirit while obscuring a secular reality that assumes us to be subhuman by default. In the natural, it may appear that we are only temporarily altering our perceptions. A secular frame might even suggest lunacy, a psychotic break from reality. Both of these perspectives reveal traditional academic frames' commitment to the erasure of religiospiritual Black women's efficacy and intellectual credence. Womanist theology and scholarly rearing make our acts of spiritual self-deliverance legible (Anzaldúa, 1981).

Our testimonies also reveal the applicability of religiospiritual women's practices to justice work. From our particular subjectivities, we produce techniques that enact social justice under some of the most difficult academic conditions. Our lives highlight the significance of faith in liberation and the problematics of framing resistance as only natural. These secular frames deny the very real emotional and spiritual toll discrimination has on the oppressed. They also deny minoritized people the opportunity to reference their own culturally specific tools as legitimate. This denial is part and parcel of religiospiritual Black women's erasure. In this exposition, we actively resist. We honor our love-centered vision of justice.

Conclusion

The present treatise counters conceptions of justice work that center natural, sterile, mind-over-body-and-spirit approaches. As such, we willfully choose not to end with the same secular model of academic writing that has worked to deny us and those like us. We instead leave the reader with a spiritual invocation, a blessing and imparting . . .

> Dear Lord, we pray, that You will bless the reader with every spiritual gift, and that You will help them to see the divine in the natural. We pray that this essay, this small offering, will encourage scholars to take a spiritual turn towards freedom. YOU are the all-powerful, all-knowing, ever-present Creator and the source of all truly creative ability. It is in You that we find true justice and liberation. Give the reader the supernatural ability to resist research practices and academic endeavors that decenter Your presence and Your will, and block pathways to deliverance. Help them to honor your Spirit in all they do. We pray the reader will grow and develop in their own spirits. And through divine relationship they will be equipped to better love the Other. Amen.

References

Anzaldúa, G. (1981). Speaking in tongues: A letter to 3rd world women writers. In C. Moraga & G. Anzaldúa (Eds.), *This bridge called my back: Writings by radical women of color* (pp. 165–174). New York, NY: Kitchen Table: Women of Color Press.
Arnold, N. W. (2014). *Ordinary theologies: Religio-spirituality and the leadership of Black female principals*. New York, NY: Peter Lang.
Baszile, D. T. (2008). Beyond all reason: The pedagogical promise of critical race testimony. *Race, Ethnicity and Education, 11*(3), 251–265.
Cannon, K. (1995). *Katie's canon: Womanism and the soul of the Black community*. New York, NY: Continuum International Publishing Group.
Collins, P. H. (1990). *Black feminist thought: Knowledge, consciousness, and the politics of empowerment*. Boston, MA: Unwin Hyman, Inc.
Coulter, C. A., & Smith, M. L. (2009). The construction zone: Literary elements in narrative research. *Educational Researcher, 38*(8), 577–590.

Cozart, S. C. (2010). When the Spirit shows up: An autoethnography of spiritual reconcil-iation with the academy. *Educational Studies, 46,* 250–269.

Crenshaw, K. (1991). Mapping the margins: Intersectionality, identity politics, and violence against women of color. *Stanford Law Review, 43*(6), 1241–1299.

Dillard, C. (2012). *Learning to (re)member the things we've learned to forget.* New York, NY: Peter Lang.

Edwards, K. T., & Baszile, D. T. (2016). Scholarly rearing in three acts: Black women's testi-monial scholarship and the cultivation of radical Black female inter-subjectivity. *Knowl-edge Cultures, 4*(1), 85–99.

Edwards, K. T. (2015). College teaching on sacred ground: Judeo-Christian in-fluences on Black women faculty pedagogy. *Race Ethnicity and Education.* doi: `10.1080/13613324.2015.1095177`

Edwards, K. T. (2014). Is it "Marissa" or "Michelle?" In K. J. Fasching-Varner, R. E. Reynolds, K. A. Albert, & L. L. Martin (Eds.), *Trayvon Martin, race, and American justice: Writing wrong* (pp. 93–100). Boston, MA: Sense Publishers.

Freire, P. (2007). *Pedagogy of the oppressed.* (M. B. Ramos, Trans.). New York, NY: Continuum International. (Original work published 1968)

Grant, J. (1989). *White women's Christ and Black women's Jesus: Feminist Christology and wom-anist response.* Atlanta, GA: Scholars Press.

Grant, J. (1982). Black women and the Church. In G. T. Hull, P. B. Scott, & B. Smith (Eds.), *But some of us are brave: Black women's studies* (pp. 141–152). New York, NY: Feminist Press.

Gregory, S. T. (1999). *Black women in the academy: The secrets to success and achievement.* Lanham, MD: University Press of America.

Harley, D. A. (2008). Maids of academe: African American women faculty at predominately White institutions. *Journal of African American Studies, 12*(1), 19–36.

Hayes, D. L. (1995). *Hagar's daughters: Womanist ways of being in the world.* New York, NY: Paulist Press.

Higginbotham, E. B. (1993). *Righteous discontent: The women's movement in the Black Baptist Church,* 1880–1920. Cambridge, MA: Harvard University Press.

hooks, b. (2004). Understanding patriarchy. In *The will to change: Men, masculinity, and love.* New York, NY: Atria Books.

Howard-Hamilton, M. F., Palmer, C., Johnson, S., & Kicklighter, M. (1998). Burnout and related factors: Differences between women and men in student affairs. *College Student Affairs Journal, 17*(2), 80–91.

Lincoln, C. E., & Mamiya, L. (1990). *The Black church in the African American experience.* Durham, NC: Duke University Press.

Lorde, A. (2008). The Master's tools will never dismantle the Master's house. In A. Bailey & C. Cuomo (Eds.), *The feminist philosophy reader* (pp. 49–51). New York, NY: McGraw Hill.

Maslach, C., Schaufeli, W. B., & Leiter, M. P. (2001). Job burnout. *Annual Review of Psychol-ogy, 52*(1), 397–422.

McKittrick, K. (2006). *Demonic grounds: Black women and the cartographies of struggle.* Min-neapolis, MN: University of Minnesota Press.

Miller, D. W. (2003). The faith at work movement. *Theology Today, 60*(3), 301–310.

Munin, A., & Speight, S. L. (2010). Factors influencing the ally development of college students. *Equity & Excellence, 43*(2), 249–264.

Ng-A-Fook, N. (2007). *An indigenous curriculum of place: The United Houma Nation's con-tentious relationship with Louisiana's educational institutions.* New York, NY: Peter Lang.

Reason, R. D., & Broido, E. M. (2005). Issues and strategies for social justice allies (and the student affairs professionals who hope to encourage them). In R. D. Reason, E. M. Broido, T. L. Davis, & N. J. Evans (Eds.), *New Directions for Student Services: No. 110. Special issue: Developing social justice allies* (pp. 81–89). San Francisco, CA: Jossey-Bass.

Tisdell, E. J. (2003). *Exploring spirituality and culture in adult and higher education.* San Francisco, CA: Jossey-Bass.

Walker, A. (1983). *In search of our mothers' gardens.* Orlando, FL: Harcourt.

Watt, S. K. (2003). Come to the river: Using spirituality to cope, resist, and develop identity. In M. F. Howard-Hamilton (Ed.), *New Directions for Student Services No. 104. Meeting the needs of African American women* (pp. 29–40). San Francisco, CA: Jossey-Bass.

KIRSTEN T. EDWARDS, PhD, is an assistant professor of adult and higher education in the Department of Educational Leadership and Policy Studies (core affiliate faculty Women's & Gender Studies and Center for Social Justice), Jeannine Rainbolt College of Education, University of Oklahoma.

VALERIE J. THOMPSON is a doctoral student in adult and higher education in the Department of Educational Leadership and Policy Studies at the University of Oklahoma.

New Directions for Adult and Continuing Education • DOI: 10.1002/ace

5

This chapter, based on the literature and interviews with both Indigenous and non-Indigenous participants, explores how land-based spirituality is at the core of Indigenous societies globally. In this chapter, an Indigenous philosophy carries a message that spirituality is not only about one's inward journey but is also about creating a better world for all.

Spirituality: The Core of Healing and Social Justice from an Indigenous Perspective

Cyndy Baskin

In the early 2000s, when I began to write and publish about spirituality in the helping professions, education and transformative change, there were few scholars, let alone Indigenous ones, who were publishing in this area (Baskin, 2002). Over a decade later, I am encouraged by the amount of information I find. Clearly, spirituality is emerging as an area of interest within many professions. I would like to think that such interest in spirituality also means that we are listening to the needs of those we serve, work with, and teach. I also believe that this interest in spirituality means that we are beginning to see people and the world around us in more holistic ways, a view that has been influenced by Indigenous worldviews. Why the rising interest in spirituality? Authors such as Zapf (2005) argue that this interest is due to the fact that the Western mindset of individualism and materialism is not working for many people anymore. Many are realizing that spirituality that encompasses connections to others, to community, and to the land may bring some meaning and fulfillment into their lives and work.

Defining Spirituality

Over the years, disciplines such as social work and religious studies have remained consistent and similar in their definitions of spirituality as encompassing an individual's values, relationships with others, and a perception of the sacred (Baskin, 2011, 2016; Canda, 1989; Gilbert, 2000; O'Rourke, 1997; Pellebon & Anderson, 1999; Zapf, 2005). Although challenging to articulate, spirituality is about wholeness, making meaning and creating inner peace. It is a sense of being at one with both one's inner and outer worlds. According to Evan Senreich (2013), a professor of social work at New York University:

New Directions for Adult and Continuing Education, no. 152, Winter 2016 © 2016 Wiley Periodicals, Inc.
Published online in Wiley Online Library (wileyonlinelibrary.com) • DOI: 10.1002/ace.20212

> Spirituality refers to a human being's subjective relationship (cognitive, emo-
> tional, and intuitive) to what is unknowable about existence, and how a person
> integrates that relationship into a perspective about the universe, the world,
> others, self, moral values, and one's sense of meaning. (p. 553)

Such a definition, although inclusive, may be troubling for those who believe
they know about the nature of our existence, where we come from and where
our spirits/souls go when the body dies. Thus, it is important to be mindful of
our language when discussing spirituality and allow those we come into contact with to provide their particular beliefs, even though they may be somewhat
different from our own.

Although religion can be a part of spirituality, religion and spirituality are
not interchangeable. And, despite scholars from diverse disciplines working
on a definition for over a century, no one definition has ever been produced
that pleases everyone (Brodd et al., 2013). In their recent work, Brodd et al.
(2013) decided on this definition of religion: "it is a cultural system integrating
teachings, practices, modes of experience, institutions, and artistic expressions
that relates people to what they perceive to be transcendent" (p. 9). The significant difference between religion and spirituality is that religion is a structured
form of spirituality that usually has a group following, whereas spirituality
can include individual experiences with or without a structured belief system
(Baskin, 2002; 2011, 2016).

Joanne Dallaire, a Cree Elder, who lives in Toronto, Ontario, Canada and
is one of my spiritual teachers, sees spirituality as a relationship with what one
believes. She shares that:

> There is a sense or connection to community through spirituality. Spirituality
> brings people together which is wanted and needed by all people. It is a way of
> expressing the self. Spirituality can create a bigger trust of the self. It is a process
> of going inward to look for answers. Spiritual practices are designed to heal in
> many cultures of the world. It is humanity's quest to seek things spiritual; to have
> something outside of the self to believe in, to help explain things that happen.
> (J. Dallaire, personal communication, July 23, 2015)

Indigenous Spirituality Is Land-Based Spirituality

My understanding of Indigenous spirituality, according to the teachings that
have been passed on to me, is that spirituality embodies an interconnectedness
and interrelationship with all life. Everyone and everything (both "animate"
and "inanimate") are seen as being equal and interdependent, part of the great
whole and as having a spirit. This view permeates the entire Indigenous vision
of life, land, and the universe.

Within Indigenous worldviews and spirituality, there is no separation
between people and the land. Place, or the physical environment, shapes
Indigenous people's entire lives and everyone else's lives as well, even though

New Directions for Adult and Continuing Education • DOI: 10.1002/ace

in Western worldviews, people are largely removed and unaware of the connections between themselves and the physical environment in which they live. Place or physical environment directly influences cultures, education, relationships, food security, transportation, and spiritual beliefs. Around the globe, there are sacred physical places that groups of people fight to protect and where they conduct their ceremonies, such as Dreamers' Rock in Ontario, Canada; the Black Hills of South Dakota, United States; Uluru (Ayers Rock) in Australia; Mecca in Saudi Arabia; the Tomb of the Virgin Mary in Kidron Valley, Jerusalem; and Potala Palace in Tibet. The Earth is often referred to as our Mother for she gives birth to us and provides all that we need. The land has the ability to calm and restore us and to inspire creativity. The land is home. The land is in us. The land is us.

I am originally from a tiny community on the Atlantic coast of Canada but currently live in Toronto, Ontario. It is the land that I miss the most: the contrast of woods and fields, the smell of the salt from the ocean, my feet sinking in the sand, and the ocean itself that goes on forever. As soon as I step onto the beach down home, my breathing begins to slow down, my muscles relax, and calmness begins. This physical state is not what I typically feel in myself and those around me as I go about my daily life in the city of Toronto, a place that always pushes at me to go faster and do more.

My best writing happens when I am on the land and water. I am able to tap into my creativity more easily. I have fewer distractions. I do everything at a slower and more thoughtful place. I feel as though I am as much a part of the environment as the chipmunks who befriend me. It is not merely that the beauty of my surroundings inspires me to write, but that my connection to place takes over and allows access to what I am *supposed* to be writing. My writing is part of my spirituality.

Of course, there is land everywhere, even under the cement of cities, because concrete is, in part, made of sand, water, and rock. Indigenous spirituality goes with us wherever we go. It teaches that a person is a spiritual being and can practice spirituality anywhere. Spirituality is inside us, in a tree in a park, a flower in a garden, and the sunset at the end of each day. Land-based ceremony, meditation, and prayer can happen every day in cities if we want it to.

Seminal writings, such as those of Hunkpapa Lakota scholar Vine Deloria Jr. (1999) and Tewa scholar Gregory Cajete (1994), explain the differences between Western society's view of nature and that of Indigenous Peoples. Deloria notes that Western society can "attribute to the landscape only the aesthetic and not the sacred perspective" because it relates to the environment through technology such as photography or television (p. 257) and Cajete writes about society's "cosmological disconnection from the natural world" (p. 25). In contrast, in Indigenous worldviews, culture, well-being, and spirituality are directly tied to one's relationship to the land. Marc Fonda (2011), senior research manager of the Strategic Research Directorate of the Ministry of Indigenous Affairs and Northern Development Canada, highlights:

> there is broad agreement that being out of the community and on the land has a rejuvenating effect on mid and body. People use hunting, camping and fishing as ways to regain a sense of well-being. Lack of access to the land may cause feelings of distress, disorientation and anxiety. To the Inuit of Canada's north [for example], the environment is not an impersonal, inanimate landscape. (p. 2)

Spirituality One on One

I have always found it confusing that professionals in the helping and healing fields are expected to assess multiple areas of a person's life, including whether a person has experienced physical and/or sexual abuse as a child or has a substance misuse challenge, yet shy away from exploring spiritual beliefs. Why is it easier to ask a person if they have been sexually abused than to ask if they believe in a creator or follow spiritual beliefs? Mohawk scholar and educator, Ruth Koleszar-Green provides an explanation for this within the context of education:

> Students are not taught to ask those they come into contact with about their spiritual beliefs or even to ask if this is a space where an individual or family can draw strength in a time of struggle.
>
> Spirituality can bring people from marginalized spaces together. No one should have to park their spirituality at the classroom door, but rather should be able to bring their whole selves in. (R. Koleszar-Green, personal communication, November 26, 2015)

Spirituality is also a major aspect of Koleszar-Green's role as a member of the Aboriginal Legal Services of Toronto's Community Council, which is an alternative to the criminal justice system for Indigenous people in conflict with the law. As she sees it:

> Council members see people through eyes with love and respect. The Council creates a space where people can begin to connect with community and with their spirituality. Many of the people who come though the Council have not had Aboriginal spirituality in their lives and state that they feel disconnected from it and the community. For many people, being through the Council has been the best thing that's happened to them as it has helped them to connect, to belong, and to be a part of something that is so much bigger than them as individuals. Spirituality heals. (R. Koleszar-Green, personal communication, November 26, 2015)

Spirituality in the Big Picture

Because spirituality encompasses everything in our lives, it cannot be seen only as an inward journey. As important as this is to an individual's source of peace, well-being, and strength, each of us has a responsibility to use our spirituality in creating a better world. How I value my life and how I value others, and how I, through this, create a life in which I can be valuable to my community and to the world is the connection that explains my existence. This connection and its emphasis on spirituality are succinctly explained by Kurt Alan Ver Beek (2000), who writes: "A sick child, dying livestock, or the question of whether to participate in risky social action are spiritual as well as physical problems, requiring both prayer and action" (p. 33). Ver Beek's (2000) description of Lenca "pilgrims" marching, "singing religious songs . . . and blowing on their conch shells—all traditional means of calling villagers to worship" (p. 33) reminds me of my own community's spiritual and holistic approach to social justice action. When Indigenous Peoples engage in social justice activities, our Elders, prayers, medicines, songs, sacred fire, and the drum are always present as sanctions of the spiritual importance of the activities.

Indigenous Peoples also have allies within the social change movement. Ver Beek (2000) writes about a large group of priests that support the Lenca through their use of "scripture, tradition and their 'pulpits' to frame the pilgrimage as a spiritual responsibility" (p. 34). This action is, of course, embedded in Catholicism's liberation theology, which emphasizes changing larger economic and political structures, rather than merely changing individuals (Dudley & Helfgott, 1990). Liberation theology is a form of optimism in which hope plays a critical role. "Hope is oriented toward the liberation and freedom of the poor, the marginalized, the exploited, the oppressed, the insignificant, or the despised in capitalist society" (Zhixiong & Rowland, 2013, p. 181) of which Indigenous Peoples the world over are certainly a part.

I like the term "a spirituality of resistance" because, for me, it links my individual and community spirituality to social justice. It brings into focus an action-oriented take on spirituality. This is in keeping with the teachings of a holistic approach to viewing a person. The spiritual aspect of me is always present. It does not come and go depending on whatever activity I am involved in. If I am participating in a spiritual ceremony, presenting to policy analysts on the racist principles of child welfare legislation or protesting with my sisters on the disappearance and murder of over 1,100 Indigenous women in Canada over the past 20 years, I am doing so with the direction and strength of the spiritual part of myself. The spirit is just as influential as the mind, body, and emotions in the work that I choose to do. This helps me understand that my spirituality is not meant to simply make me feel better in times of distress. Rather, it is what pushes me forward in understanding, resisting, and taking action toward social justice for all of humanity.

Spirituality as responsibility, then, involves resisting the evil in this world. The evil is oppression and all that it entails in its harm to all creatures of the

Earth and the Earth herself. This resistance has always been present in the lives of spiritual people. Historically, for prophets, "a spiritual form of life had to include responsiveness to the hunger or anguish of those around us, as well as seeing and resisting the authority of the arrogant and privileged who controlled the kingdom" (Gottlieb, 1999, p. 26). There have been more recent resistors, such as Martin Luther King Jr., Gandhi, and Malcolm X. There have also been Indigenous leaders who have resisted colonization, for example, Crazy Horse, Louis Riel, Leonard Peltier, and a group of women who were imprisoned in the infamous women's prison in Kingston, Ontario, Canada who created songs about the strengths of women.

Spirituality Connects Us All

Peggy Wilson (as cited in Steinhauer, 2002) relates a story about how, before the Exxon Valdez oil spill that occurred in Prince William Sound, Alaska in 1989, one of her students had a dream in which everything was black, and she felt like she was being strangled by this black mass. The student was moved and shocked into action by this experience because her dream took place the night before the oil spill. This was one of the most horrendous environmental catastrophes to date with scientists estimating in 2014 that between 16,000 and 21,000 gallons of oil remained on the beaches in Prince William Sound and up to 450 miles away (Walters, 2014, March 23). The student wondered if anyone else in the world had had that warning. She placed an ad in a number of newspapers throughout the world. She received responses from as far away as England and Africa with people describing similar dreams before that monumental disaster. She referred to this experience as the collective unconscious (Steinhauer, 2002, pp. 75–76). Experiences such as this one send a clear message: we are all connected. Regardless of how we explain such phenomena, whether we refer to them as the collective unconsciousness or spirituality, the Earth ties us together.

Commonalities

I found countless examples of commonalities among the spirituality of Indigenous Peoples on Turtle Island, New Zealand, Tibet, and the continent of Africa, to name a few. I have also learned about these similarities from relatives, friends, and students. My brother-in-law, who is originally from Mozambique, and I have shared many stories about our worldviews. Our worldviews are similar in their focus on community values rather than individual interests and on the importance of ceremony for one's well-being. We have similar understandings about the drum, language, and the healing properties of plants, despite the fact that we grew up on opposite sides of the world.

In fact, Afrocentricity, like Indigenous worldviews, is described as relying on spirituality, appreciating the connectedness of all on the planet and in the cosmos, emphasizing the collective rather than the individual and promoting

New Directions for Adult and Continuing Education • DOI: 10.1002/ace

harmony among all. The teachings are oral, there is a belief in a creator and spirits, honor of the ancestors, and the use of traditional medicines, as well as the role of human beings to harmonize nature with the spirits (Asante, 2009). African American scholar, Mambo Ama Mazama (2002) writes that within diverse African forms of spirituality, "special rituals take place before cutting trees down" (p. 220), which is exactly what happens on Turtle Island as well. Mazama (2002) speaks of the connection between human beings and the spirit world, noting that "the ancestors provide guidance; they will send us messages about how we operate in this life, in this world, if we honor them" (p. 222). We are more alike than we are different!

The use of the circle is also prominent in the helping and healing practices of Indigenous Peoples, as well as within leadership, throughout Africa and North America.

Mazama (2002) states that the circle "is the African symbol par excellence" (p. 221). Two examples of African-based approaches that focus on the spiritual energy of the circle are the story circle technique (Garrett et al., 2008) and the dance of the ring shout (Garrett et al., 2008; Powell, 2013). These approaches offer support to the members of the circle through connectedness and belonging. Similar to the methods of many Indigenous groups on Turtle Island, these approaches help participants to connect with themselves, the world around them and the ancestors who came before them (Garrett et al., 2008; Powell, 2013).

Another spiritual practice common to many of the Earth's people is meditation. Kabat-Zinn (2005) explains why mindfulness meditation has spread across the planet:

> The systematic cultivation of mindfulness has been called the heart of Buddhist meditation . . . In recent years, the practice of this kind of meditation has become widespread in the world. Although at this time, mindfulness meditation is most commonly taught and practiced within the context of Buddhism, its essence is universal. (p. 12)

Thirteen Grandmothers: Spirituality Can Heal Our World

At this point in our history, it is beyond doubt that we are living amidst an environmental catastrophe whereby humans are slowly killing the Earth and ourselves. We are being warned through climate change and the increasingly frequent and catastrophic "natural disasters" that are taking place around the globe. The industrial and agricultural practices that exploit both the physical environment and human beings are supported by the values and beliefs of a Western society that believes that economic well-being, which often translates into having more things and gaining material wealth, will lead to overall well-being. In other words, materialism and consumerism equals happiness. These beliefs also stress that technology will solve all of our problems. However, the kinds of material benefits that these claims support are not within reach of 80% of the Earth's population, nor is our current rate of consumption sustainable (Brown, 2014; Chossudovsky, 1998; Gottlieb, 2013; Wackernagel & Rees, 1995). Overproduction in the name of progress has generated both horrendous pollution and increasing human exploitation as people engage in low paid and often dangerous subsistence wage jobs struggle to keep up with an increasing demand for products.

Carol Schaefer (2006) has published a beautiful collection of female Indigenous Elders' teachings about how Indigenous knowledges can heal the world. Later, in 2009, a film was created about the grandmothers called, *For the Next 7 Generations: 13 Indigenous Grandmothers Weaving a World that Works* (Hart & Hart, 2009). Thirteen Grandmothers from the Arctic, North, South, and Central America, Africa, Tibet, and Nepal have been coming together to speak about "ways of bringing about sustainability, sovereignty, and a united alliance among all the Earth's people" (Schaefer, 2006, p. 8). These Grandmothers are following a Hopi (Indigenous Nation whose territory is in northeastern Arizona) prophecy that states that people from the four directions must come together before there can be peace on the Earth. They are fulfilling this prophecy by coming together with their teachings and healing methods for the first time in history, in order to find ways of creating a better world (Schaefer, 2006). These Grandmothers have also met with Western women Elders. Their humility, generosity, and love for all of humanity is expressed by Schaefer (2006) who writes, "Prophecy revealed to each one that they must now share even their most secret and sacred ways with the very people who have been their oppressors, as the survival of humanity, if not the entire planet, is at stake" (p. 4).

Omyene Grandmother Bernadette Rebienot of Gabon, Africa explains why the Earth is in such turmoil. She states that because male energies across the world are in control, power cannot be balanced because women's influence is undermined and their wisdom and access to feminine energy is often cut off (Schaefer, 2006). Everything in the world is connected, including politics and consciousness. The Grandmothers are certain that women will show us a different way of being in this world. This group of women Elders encourage all of us to do our personal healing as this is a necessary first step to healing the world. These Elders emphasize that people need to resolve the conflicts they have within themselves in order to see how we unconsciously create damage to our world.

The Grandmothers also speak about forgiveness, releasing the past and letting go of judgments. Yupik Elder Rita Pitka Blumenstien of Alaska tells us that when we do this, "we give ourselves permission to define ourselves, rather than being defined by others or past events. We are free to become who we are" (as cited in Schaefer, 2006, p. 142). The Grandmothers tell us that it is women's wisdom that will save the world. Women need to build alliances and share their wisdom. When women come together in circles, they can awaken the wisdom in each other's hearts and spirits. This hope is expressed by Grandmother Agnes Baker Pilgrim of the Takelma Siletz Nation in Oregon:

New Directions for Adult and Continuing Education • DOI: 10.1002/ace

It is my hope that the Grandmothers' Council will have a mushroom effect throughout the world. That women will start circling up, come together, and bond together, to help one another to be better and stand tall with their voices, to say they've had enough of oppression. It is my hope that they will form matriarchal bridges with each other and be a voice again for our Mother Earth and Her children. (Schaefer, 2006, p. 143)

Conclusion

The strongest leaders in the history of the world have been those who practice spirituality as a regular part of their everyday lives. These are the ones who have touched the spirit of those around them, as well as those they have never met, in the leading of social justice movements that focus on love for all. If human beings continue to destroy our Mother the Earth, the color of one's skin or the amount of money in one's bank account is not going to matter. If She dies, we all die. We are living in a time where we have no choice but to explore more spiritual ways of educating, nurturing, and supporting leadership that will literally change the world as we know it.

References

Asante, M. K. (2009). *Encyclopedia of African religion*. Thousand Oaks, CA: Sage.

Baskin, C. (2002). Circles of resistance: Spirituality in social work practice, education and transformative change. *Currents: New Scholarship in the Human Services*. Retrieved from http://www.ucalgary.ca/currents/files/currents/v1n1_baskin.pdf

Baskin, C. (2011). *Strong helpers' teachings: The value of Indigenous knowledges in the helping professions*. Toronto: Canadian Scholars' Press.

Baskin, C. (2016). *Strong helpers' teachings: The value of Indigenous knowledges in the helping Professions* (2nd ed.). Toronto: Canadian Scholars' Press.

Brodd, J., Little, L., Nystrom, B., Platzner, R., Shek, R., & Stiles, E. (2013). *Invitation to world religions*. New York: Oxford University Press.

Brown, P. J. (2014). Religion and global health. In E. L. Idler (Ed.), *Religion as a social determinant of public health* (pp. 273–297). New York: Oxford University Press.

Cajete, G. (1994). *Look to the mountain: An ecology of Indigenous education*. Durango: Kivaki Press.

Canda, E. (1989). Religious content in social work education: A comparative approach. *Journal of Social Work Education, 25*(1), 36–45.

Chossudovsky, M. (1998). *The globalisation of poverty*. Halifax: Fernwood.

Deloria, V., Jr. (1999). *For this land: Writings of religion in America*. New York: Routledge.

Dudley, J., & Helfgott, C. (1990). Exploring a place for spirituality in the social work curriculum. *Journal of Social Work Education, 26*(3), 287–293.

Fonda, M. (2011). Traditional knowledge, spirituality and lands. *International Indigenous Policy Journal, 2*(4). Retrieved from http://ir.lib.uwo.ca/iipj/vol2/iss4/1

Garrett, M., Brubaker, M., Torres-Rivera, E., West-Olatunji, C., & Conwill, W. L. (2008). The medicine of coming to center: Use of the Native American centering technique—Ayeli—to promote wellness and healing in group work. *Journal for Specialists in Group Work, 33*(2), 179–198. doi:10.1080/01933920801977322

Gilbert, M. C. (2000). Spirituality in social work groups: Practitioners speak out. *Social Work with Groups, 22*(4), 67–84. doi:10.1300/J009v22n04_06

Gottlieb, R. S. (1999). *A spirituality of resistance*. New York: Crossroad Publishing.

Gottlieb, R. S. (2013). *Spirituality: What it is and why it matters*. New York: Oxford University Press.

Hart, C. (Producer), Hart, C., & Hart, B. (Directors). (2009). *For the next 7 generations: 13 Indigenous grandmothers weaving a world that works* [Motion Picture]. USA: The Laughing Willow Company.

Kabat-Zinn, J. (2005). *Full catastrophe living: Using the wisdom of your body and mind to face stress, pain, and illness*. New York: Bantam Dell.

Mazama, M. A. (2002). Afrocentricity and African spirituality. *Journal of Black Studies, 33*(2), 218–234. Retrieved from http://www.jstor.org

O'Rourke, C. (1997). Listening for the sacred: Addressing spiritual issues in the group treatment of adults with mental illness. *Smith College Studies in Social Work, 67*(2), 177–195.

Pellebon, D. A., & Anderson, S. C. (1999). Understanding the life issues of spiritually-based clients. *Families in Society, 80*(3), 229–239. `doi:10.1606/1044-3894.676`

Powell, A. (2013). African American ring shouts (origins & examples). *Pancocojams*. Retrieved from http://pancocojams.blogspot.ca/2013/05/african-american-ring-shouts-origins.html

Schaefer, C. (2006). *Grandmothers counsel the world: Women elders offer their wisdom for our planet*. Boston: Trumpeter Books.

Senreich, E. (2013). An inclusive definition of spirituality for social work education and practice. *Journal of Social Work Education, 49*, 548–563. `doi:10.1080/10437797.2013.812460`

Steinhauer, E. (2002). Thoughts on an Indigenous methodology. *Canadian Journal of Native Education, 26*(2), 69–81.

Ver Beek, K. (2000). Spirituality: A developmental taboo. *Development in Practice, 10*(1), 31–43.

Wackernagel, M., & Rees, W. (1995). *Our ecologist footprint: Reducing human impact on the earth*. Gabriola Island, BC: New Society Publishers.

Walters, J. (2014, March 23). Exxon Valdez—25 years after the Alaska oil spill, the court battle continues. *The Telegraph*. Retrieved from http://www.telegraph.co.uk/news/worldnews/northamerica/usa/10717219/Exxon-Valdez-25-years-after-the-Alaska-oil-spill-the-court-battle-continues.html

Zapf, M. K. (2005). The spiritual dimension of person and environment: Perspectives from social work and traditional knowledge. *International Social Work, 48*(5), 633–642. `doi:10.1177/0020872805055328`

Zhixiong, L., & Rowland, C. (2013). Hope: The convergence and divergence of Marxism and liberation theology. *Theology Today, 70*(2), 181–195. `doi:10.1177/0040573613484752`

CYNDY BASKIN is associate professor, School of Social Work, and chair, Aboriginal Education Council, Ryerson University, Toronto, Ontario.

6

In this chapter, we reconnect with and reflect on our own stories of working within a university setting and how we create spaces for the possibility of transformative learning. Through this process, we have renewed our purpose to advocate for a deeper focus on "the relational" in those contexts where a dominant focus on systems, structures, and processes marginalize the needs and voices of those who work and learn within them.

Creating Spaces for Transformative Learning in the Workplace

Janet Groen, Colleen Kawalilak

What happens when you intentionally slow things down in the workplace so people have a chance to engage in dialogue and really connect with each other? If we engage in this way, we may go deeper and begin to ask different questions about our workplaces, such as: What are we doing? Why are we doing this? Why are we approaching things in this way? In other words, we open the possibility for change when we lift up our heads and stop "just doing." However, we are becoming aware that we have fallen into the "doing" trap; working as academics with heads down, to address an insatiable list of demands. This quest to "keep up" was reinforced when a colleague sent us a link to a webpage that offered advice on how to work differently. What struck us was that the focus was on individual strategies and techniques: ways and means to cope within the workplace common to many of us who work within higher education. This is a setting where we are barraged with committee meetings, email requests, writing reference letters for students, and other unending tasks. Again, what if we slowed down, connected with each other in dialogue, and began to really talk? It is in this space that we open up the possibility to go deeper, moving beyond coping mechanisms to question underlying structures in support of contributing to workplace environments and cultures that are more just and caring.

Underlying the ideas of slowing things down, dialoguing, and connecting is our belief that these are indeed spiritual processes. Drawing from Tisdell's (2003) work, we suggest that spirituality is about being aware and honoring the wholeness and interconnectedness of all things through the mystery of a higher power. It is about seeking a sense of purpose and ultimately making

NEW DIRECTIONS FOR ADULT AND CONTINUING EDUCATION, no. 152, Winter 2016 © 2016 Wiley Periodicals, Inc.
Published online in Wiley Online Library (wileyonlinelibrary.com) • DOI: 10.1002/ace.20213

meaning in one's life. The potential for connectivity with spirituality is always present in the learning environment. It is also about how people construct knowledge through largely unconscious and symbolic processes. As well, we believe that spirituality is about action and an outward response that challenges inequities, works toward social justice, and asks difficult and uncomfortable questions.

In this chapter, we reconnect to and reflect on our own stories of working within the university and how we create spaces for the possibility of transformative learning. By reconnecting with our own stories and with each other through dialogue, we have a renewed belief in the importance of advocating for a focus on "the relational" in contexts where a dominant focus on systems, structures, and processes marginalizes the needs and voices of those who work and learn within them.

Connecting the Autobiographical with Cultural Context

Over the years, we have each taken up positions providing us opportunities to create those spaces—not only within our teaching but also as chairs of programs and committees, and having assumed larger portfolios as senior leaders in our school of education. Focused on intentionally slowing down the pace and interrupting the scurry of activity, we aim to create spaces in support of the emergence of opportunities for reflection, dialogue, and a substantial conversation about how we might change things around us.

Autoethnography supports the creation of space for reflection and dialogue as "research, writing, story, and method that connect[s] the autobiographical and personal to the cultural, social, and political" (Ellis, 2004, p. xix). Understood as a co-constructed narrative, autoethnographies have the potential to illuminate "relationships between people, [relationships that are] jointly authored, incomplete, and historically situated. Connections hinge on contingencies of conversation and negotiation that often produce unexpected outcomes" (p. 71). Autoethnography and dialogue share a common essence in that both support and inform narrative learning aimed to explore and gain a deeper understanding of perspective and lived experience. Connecting autoethnography to dialogue, Ellis and Bochner (2000) referred to the capacity of stories to:

> inspire conversation from the point of view of the readers [and listeners], who enter from the perspective of their own lives. The narrative rises or falls on it capacity to provoke [others] to broaden their horizons, reflect critically on their own experience, enter empathetically into worlds of experience different from their own and actively engage in dialogue regarding the social and moral implications of the different perspectives and standpoints encountered. (p. 748)

Sharing stories of our own experiences and listening to one another's ponderings served as a catalyst to reflect on held perspectives, assumptions, and insights gained, having navigated the cultural, contextual, and often challenging landscape of academia for almost one and a half decades.

Voices from the Literature

Discourses of transformative learning and spirituality and adult learning, although not being synonymous, are often intertwined. For example, even though research into transformative learning, briefly defined as a deep shift in the way people see themselves in relation to the world around them (Clark, 1993; Cranton & King, 2003), came first, we can see how it became a doorway into some of the initial exploration on spirituality and adult learning. For example, Dirkx (1997) in his critique of the analytic, reflective, and rational processes of transformation outlined by Mezirow (1981, 1991), in the early years of his research in this area, introduced the notion of soul and spirit into this particular pathway of learning. "Transformative learning also involves very personal and imaginative ways of knowing. . . . Our journey of self-knowledge also requires that we care for and nurture the presence of the soul dimension in teaching and learning" (Dirkx, 1997, p. 80).

Notable as well was a broadening of our understanding of both transformative learning and spirituality and adult learning beyond the individual to incorporate an outward focus on learning for social justice. For example, English and Gillen (2000) stated that spirituality has two dimensions: "one marked by withdrawal from the world and the other marked by immersion in the world. The latter distinction, which is characterized by a social and political dimension is what interests us as adult educators" (p. 1). As well, English and Tisdell (2010), reinforcing this dual focus, felt that, although spirituality and learning are about connecting to meaning and a divine being, "it requires the individual to reach out to the world in search of justice and right living" (English & Tisdell cited in English, 2012, p. 21). In turn, a holistic understanding of transformative learning offered by O'Sullivan (2002) also involves a shift of consciousness that reaches beyond the individual. This includes "our understanding of relations of power in interlocking structures of class, race, and gender; our body-awareness; our visions of alternative approaches to living; and our sense of the possibilities for social justice and peace and personal joy" (O'Sullivan, 2002, p. 11)

Narrowing our focus to the workplace context, we see the emphasis of spirituality and learning, as well as transformative learning, is about individual wellness, creativity, and meaning *and* about social justice. Although some organizational and workplace learning literature (Biberman & Tischler, 2008; Neal & Biberman, 2004) suggested that there are tremendous benefits to promoting spirituality in the workplace, other early researchers (Fenwick & Lange, 1998; Mitroff & Denton, 1999) were cautious about this trend. They wondered about the motivations of organizations that saw this as the latest strategy in order to achieve better results or to increase the profit margins, and argued that it must be practiced for its own sake. As English (2012) rightly indicated, there is the possibility that spirituality in the workplace can become so watered down that it might serve as a catchall for notions of creativity, happiness, empowerment, and engagement. "The threat of over-spiritualizing the work world is a real one, since it has the potential to erode personal boundaries and spaces ... the only defensible purpose for acknowledging or cultivating spirituality of workers ought to be for providing assistance for human flourishing" (p. 27). It is in this space, where spirituality and adult learning and transformative learning can offer significant value. When we probe the underlying structures within our workplaces and consider if and how we are supported, it is here where we may bump against unethical and dehumanizing practices that undermine our ability to thrive.

Guided by Our Own Narratives

And so as we turn to approaches that offer the potential to unearth and challenge these practices within our workplaces, a pivotal learning process that is highlighted in both transformative learning and spirituality and adult learning is dialogue. Turning first to transformative learning, Taylor (2009) believed that dialogue is a core part of this process of learning and it "becomes the medium for critical reflections to be put into actions" (p. 9). In turn, dialogue is an enactment of a pivotal spiritual value: interconnectedness.

Janet's Narrative. It is hard to believe, but it has already been 14 years since I defended my doctoral dissertation titled *The Practice and Experience of Adult Educators in Addressing the Spiritual Dimensions of Their Workplace* (Groen, 2002). I remember, as I spent time with my participants, I began to realize how encompassing spirituality within the workplace could be. Although I had already intuited that it could focus on the individual and the "fulfillment of vocation and creativity" (Groen & Kawalilak, 2006), my study also revealed that its outward manifestation in cultivating interconnectedness moved beyond a sense of community with our colleagues, to work toward ethical operational practices and decision-making practices. Turning to learning approaches and avenues used to guide these adult educators, it became apparent that nobody set out to deliberately create moments or spaces that could be described as "spiritual." And yet, they all described times when, through the processes of dialogue and storytelling, they felt something had shifted in the group. "There are moments of grace where, the only way I can make the difference between the small "g" and the big "G" is that something else is there. The whole becomes greater than the sum of the parts. Something takes flight" (Groen, 2004, p. 19).

And so here we are 14 years later, when across the distance of time, my dissertation seems almost prophetic in its findings and recommendations, so much so that a myriad of feelings washed over me as I flipped through the pages. It seemed like there was so much distance between the ideals of my study and the current reality of my own workplace here at the university! However, rather than only looking outward to assign responsibility, I am challenging myself to determine if there are places and spaces, where I, now a

New Directions for Adult and Continuing Education • DOI: 10.1002/ace

more senior scholar and mentor, enact the transformative potential of spirituality in the workplace. I ask this because Colleen and I, early in our academic careers, realized the importance of a particular type of senior mentor in helping us along the way: "We were the beneficiaries of these academic who believed in and had a passion for the vocation here, and wanted to help us navigate the challenges and intricacies of new workplace culture" (Groen & Kawalilak, 2006, p. 67).

Now, we are those senior mentors who attend and lead multiple meetings. It is in this space that I offer an example of cultivating the possibility for transformative learning within my workplace. This past year, there came the opportunity to apply for a small internal grant to intentionally gather colleagues within our faculty to explore shared research interests—in our case, environmental education and pedagogy in Alberta.

In preparing for that first meeting, I knew I wanted it to be a "different" gathering. Having just returned from a 6-month sabbatical, I was shocked at the rapid pace of the academy and was increasingly distressed by most of the meetings I attended. Agendas were packed and items were driven by the overarching university goal to be more competitive in research rankings and become increasingly successful in bringing in more and larger research grants. Our treasured space could not be just another typical meeting; here was the chance to slow down, to reflect, to be vulnerable, and to engage with each other in ways that would unearth multiple ways of learning about environmental education. We started slowly, getting to know each other through stories, with our artifacts and by dialoguing and listening to each other's dreams and ideas. Through this mindful unfolding, we came to realize that this was not just an "intellectual exercise." We uncovered our emotional connection to nature—our despair at the state of our world, and an increasing anxiousness and desire "to do" something within our university, and within our local community. Paradoxically, when we revisited the expected outcomes of the collaborative research grant, we more than achieved them; we simply chose a different pathway that focused on each person and how their stories and ideas could create something of meaning and significance.

Colleen's Narrative. I defended my PhD research 2 years after Janet, on March 11, 2004. Pursuing a doctoral degree was never part of my plan. One might say I stumbled blindly into graduate school. I was navigating a monumental life transition that had taken me by surprise in that I woke up one day to realize the photograph of my life that had always occupied the picture frame in my mind was about to drastically change; my marriage was ending. In retrospect, pursuing graduate studies was my attempt to recreate a future for myself.

The days were long, the learning curve steep, and the generous support received from my supervisor and committee plentiful. There were many moments where "mature" and "rich in experience" failed to soothe my anxieties. Although I was well into my 40s and older than many, I was still younger than a few. I knew that I was exactly where I needed to be at that precise moment. As

New Directions for Adult and Continuing Education • DOI: 10.1002/ace

an eager PhD student, I was passionate about the relational aspects of learning, knowledge sharing, and knowledge co-creation.

I was inspired by deep conversations with fellow students, my supervisor, and other professors who invited me to share my perspective and experience as a doctoral student attempting to successfully navigate academia. In spite of the hectic pace that informs most work and learning environments, my time on campus also presented a welcomed "pause," a space within which to reflect on all I was learning and experiencing. Tisdell (2003) referred to the importance of critically reflecting "on one's life assumptions" (p. 124) to better understand how our spiritual development shifts, shapes, and unfolds. These spaces of pause encouraged a sharper focus in me—a deeper concentration on what constituted an authentic life and a more coherent path of work and learning as an adult educator and lifelong learner, a pathway grounded in and guided by spirituality.

These reflective moments were further supported by the cultural context within which I conducted my doctoral research—an Indigenous adult learning center and community in Western Australia. Invited by an Indigenous colleague to engage in dialogue with herself and other Indigenous Elders, we aimed to explore our *common ground* as lifelong adult learners, a place of *Oneness* believed to reside *beyond* our cultural differences. It was within this space that I learned how to listen. To be authentically present to others required a letting go agendas I held tight, all those ways I hoped to persuade others to see things from my perspective. Within this space, I was reminded of the power of relationships and how creating space for open, authentic dialogue also served as a powerful pathway for navigating tensions and dilemmas.

As I transitioned from doctoral student to assistant professor, I sought to bear witness to the power of dialogue. I deeply believed "that relationships are the *essence* and *bedrock* of [my] work [and] that [this] provide[d] me great privilege and opportunity in support of [individual and mutual] growth and development as adult educators and lifelong, adult learners" (Kawalilak & Groen, 2014, p. 35). I was forthright in my belief that creating spaces for dialogue, versus populating these spaces with agenda items and "to do" tasks would contribute to a culture and community informed by collaboration, respect, trust, and healthy discourse. One sometimes pays a price for this philosophical stance, however, in that we can be regarded as "too soft"—not tough or thick skinned enough. This was evidenced during a strategic planning session when, after being promoted to associate dean, I was asked to work with my colleagues to articulate a mission, vision, and values for our school. When a dear colleague and myself advanced the notion that treating one another with "care and compassion" be clearly addressed in our strategic plan, another colleague said that she felt this was more aligned to a "kindergarten motto" than to a higher education setting. As others in the room fell silent, I struggled to find my words. Then, with reserve and respect I said, "I am thinking that care and compassion is what we all need to grow and thrive as a community—this is something we never grow out of."

New Directions for Adult and Continuing Education • DOI: 10.1002/ace

I admit that, as part of the leadership team, there are moments when it is challenging to always respond from a stance of positive regard and grace. The pressure to fill rare and precious "spaces" with information items and a never-ending list or pending tasks thwarts intentions to not only create but sustain these spaces for dialogue.

Making Meaning of Our Stories

As we prepare to draw meaning from our respective stories, we first return to our process of engagement in preparing this article; for it was by attending to the autoethnographic and dialogic processes outlined earlier in this article that we were able unfold significant learnings. Specifically, after we each wrote our stories of our respective journeys, we met to read our stories out loud to each other. As each read her story, the other listened deeply and responded, asking questions of clarification and offering observations and thoughts. It was through this exchange that we were able to come to a deeper understanding, not only of the other's story but also of our own story. For example, Colleen, in writing her story admitted that she was feeling stuck in her doctoral journey, unable to continue into her current reality as an associate professor and associate dean. The ensuing dialogue probed the underlying conditions that caused this blockage and gradually she came to the realization that she was finding the current reality of our university to be deeply challenging. In turn, this led her to reflect on what is currently required in order bring a sense of renewal to the important contributions she is making to our workplace.

From Divided to Undivided Lives. Building on the disease that Colleen was feeling about her current engagement within the university culture, we began to realize the high toll working in a fragmented workplace culture was having on us. Demands are rapidly increasing and rarely do we experience the required sense of space and reflective engagement that is needed in order to engage in the deeply satisfying part of our work life as academics. Both of were drawn to this work because of our passion for teaching and engagement with our students, as well as focusing on research that delves into contexts and approaches to adult learning that unleash the possibility of learning where "we *all* have a role to play, in our own unique ways, in supporting the well-being of those lives we touch" (Groen & Kawalilak, 2014, p. 228).

As it currently stands, it can often feel like we are the embodiment of a divided life or a life of alteration, where we cycle through work–exhaustion–rest, work–exhaustion–rest. The writing of our individual stories and our ensuing dialogue has served as a reminder for both of us to reclaim and move forward on our pathway to lives "where meaning and purpose are tightly interwoven with intellect and action, where compassion and care are infused with insight and knowledge" (Palmer & Zajonc, 2010, p. 56). Tisdell (2011) believed that our renewed quest to live undivided lives reflects an engagement with the paradox of wisdom, where we are trying to engage in the inner and transcendent cultivation of wisdom in order to reflect a practical wisdom in our daily lives. In summary, in order to cultivate and sustain the possibility of transformative change in our workplace, we need to also be mindful of attending to our inner well-being. Janet is reminded to take up her mindfulness meditation practice again and to continue her almost daily practice of walking out in nature. Colleen is reminded to step into those sometimes uncomfortable and awkward spaces when, at team leadership meetings, it is critical to remind her good colleagues that care, compassion, and holding spaces open for being authentically open and present to one another through dialogue is not a "soft" recommendation that belongs in the margins. We need to remember that we are *not* machines and our schools and faculties are *not* factories. Rather, we are a community of lifelong learners, scholars, and professional practitioners who need to focus as heavily on the human resources—on caring for and cultivating the "relational culture" during times of change and transition, as we do on revising and *re*forming systems and structures.

We also believe, if we are to truly live undivided lives that attending to our inner well-being should not simply be taken up outside of our places of work. In a way, we are coming to realize that some of the suggestions from the Internet page that our colleague sent to us about slowing down do make sense. And yet, although they do help to contribute to an inner sense of well-being within our work, on their own, they do not go deep enough. Part of our inner well-being at work, as Palmer & Zajonc (2010) and Janet's doctoral research (Groen, 2002) found, taps into a critical dimension of spirituality; a sense of meaning and purpose. As we considered if and how our places work cultivate such a sense of meaning and purpose, that is when we began to go deeper to probe at the underlying structures and supports that either enhance or detract from this possibility.

Dialogue, as mentioned earlier, is an adult learning process we have both tapped into with great success to move into such a space. Dialogue is pivotal to both transformative learning and spirituality and learning as it offers the possibility to co-create a new way of understanding and being. Already, through the dialogue that ensured through the writing of this article, we are in each in a different space; each reflecting with renewed energy on our sense of meaning and purpose at the university as we begin to see ourselves as senior academics. In turn, we have begun to realize that there are spaces where we can be more explicit in challenging structures and systems that undermine our ability to do "good work" as faculty members.

Reflecting on Our Reflections

As we reflect on the past 12–14 years since our respective hires as assistant professors, we recognize a significant shift within our workplace culture. Having assumed an array of leadership roles within our school of education, we have each sat on many committees responsible for identifying and establishing checks and balances, action items, outcomes, and other quantitative metrics to measure performance, productivity, and overall engagement of our academic colleagues. The language of the corporate world has become commonplace within these meeting contexts and, unfortunately, this has sometimes contributed to positioning "people" and "product" in binary opposition of the other. Indeed, we are certainly not naive to the economic realities that challenge the development and delivery of programs in higher education and the increased dependency of higher education institutions on business and industry for funding and support. In light of this shift, however, we maintain that it is even *more critical* that we put forth the call for a more thoughtful, purposeful, and intentional focus on the creation of spaces that support engagement with one another as colleagues and collaborators, and a more contemplative scholarly practice.

We also resist the expectation that some might have to generate a list of "action items" designed solely to "target" particular goals, measureable objectives, and outcomes. Granted, although change will continue to impact and influence university landscapes and the work of those who work within these cultures and contexts, there are multiple ways to approach this. Although we have witnessed and been impacted by some leaders who focus heavily bringing about change through the reforming and restructuring of systems, structures, and processes, we have also experienced leaders and change agents who focus more on relational components. More specifically, these leaders draw on the spiritual processes of slowing down, dialogue, and building community to pay close attention to how members of that community authentically engage, so that faculty and staff members are not marginalized, but are empowered to be a part of the change. We believe the latter more easily and organically provide spaces for dialogue; and for building community, connectedness, expressions of care and compassion; and for transformative learning to best reside and thrive. It is important that we advocate for a deeper focus on "the relational" in those contexts where a dominant focus on systems, structures, and processes marginalize and muffle the needs and voices of those who work and learn within them. We need to empower others and ourselves to exercise some choice about the ways in which changes in higher education impact us as academics as, in the words of Peter Knight (2002), "Institutions have become 'greedy', asking for more without caring sufficiently for the humans who work in them" (p. 9). If there ever was a time for self-care and being guided by heart, it is now.

When the heart speaks, listen.

Then, respond compassionately and consistently.
Mona M. Johnson (2011, p. xv)

References

Biberman, J., & Tischler, L. (2008). Spirituality in business: Theory, practice and future directions. New York, NY: Palgrave Macmillan.

New Directions for Adult and Continuing Education • DOI: 10.1002/ace

Clark, M. (1993). Transformational learning. In S. B. Merriam (Ed.), *New Directions for Adult and Continuing: No. 57. An update on adult learning theory* (pp. 47–57). San Francisco, CA: Jossey-Bass.

Cranton, P., & King, K. (2003). Transformative learning as a professional development goal. In K. P. King & P. A. Lawler (Eds.), *New Directions for Adult and Continuing Education: No. 98. New perspectives on designing and implementing professional development of teachers of adults* (pp. 31–37). San Francisco, CA: Jossey-Bass.

Dirkx, J. (1997). Nurturing soul in adult learning. In P. Cranton (Ed.), *New Directions for Adult and Continuing Education: No. 74. Transformative learning in action: Insights from practice* (pp. 79–88). San Francisco, CA: Jossey-Bass.

Ellis, C. (2004). *The ethnographic I: A methodological novel about autoethnography*. Walnut Creek, CA: Altamira Press.

Ellis, C., & Bochner, A. P. (2000). Autoethnography, personal narrative, reflexivity. In N. K. Denzin & Y. S. Lincoln (Eds.), *Handbook of qualitative research* (2nd ed., pp. 733–768). Thousand Oaks, CA: Sage.

English, L. (2012). For whose purposes? Examining the spirituality agenda in adult education. In J. Groen, D. Coholic, & J. Graham (Eds.), *Spirituality in education and social work: Theory, practice and pedagogies* (pp. 17–33). Waterloo, ON: Wilfrid Laurier Press.

English, L. M., & Gillen, M. A. (2000). Editors' notes. In L. M. English & M. A. Gillen (Eds.), *New Directions for Adult and Continuing Education: No. 85. Addressing the spiritual dimensions of adult learning: What educators can do* (pp. 1–5). San Francisco, CA: Jossey-Bass.

English, L., & Tisdell, E. (2010). Spirituality in adult education. In C. Kasworm, A. Rose, & J. Ross-Gordon (Eds.), *Handbook of adult and continuing education* (pp. 285–293). San Francisco, CA: Jossey-Bass.

Fenwick, T., & Lange, E. (1998). Spirituality in the workplace: The new frontier of HRD. *Canadian Journal for the Study of Adult Education, 12*(1), 63–87.

Groen, J. (2002). *The experience and practice of adult educators in addressing the spiritual dimensions of the workplace* (Unpublished doctoral dissertation). University of Toronto, Canada.

Groen, J. (2004). The creation of soulful spaces: An exploration of the processes and the organizational context. *Organization Development Journal, 22*(3), 8–19.

Groen, J., & Kawalilak, C. (2006). Creating community—A "new" faculty perspective. *Organization Development Journal, 24*(1), 57–67.

Groen, J., & Kawalilak, C. (2014). *Pathways to adult learning: Professional and education narratives*. Toronto, ON: Canadian Scholars' Press.

Johnson, M. (2011). Introduction—The heart of learning. In R. Wolpow, M. Johnson, R. Hertel, & S. Kincaid (Eds.), *The heart of learning and teaching: Compassion, resiliency, and academic success* (p. 15). Olympia, WA: Washington State Office of Superintendent of Public Instruction Compassionate Schools.

Kawalilak, C., & Groen, J. (2014). An "educated heart" and teaching practice. *Journal of Educational Thought, 47*(1–2), 33–47.

Knight, P. T. (2002). *Being a teacher in higher education*. Ballmoor, Buckingham: SRHE and Open University Press.

Mezirow, J. (1981). A critical theory of adult learning and education. *Adult Education Quarterly, 32*(1), 3–24.

Mezirow, J. (1991). *Transformative dimensions of adult learning*. San Francisco, CA: Jossey-Bass.

Mitroff, I., & Denton, E. (1999). *A spiritual audit of corporate America: A hard look at spirituality, religion and values in the workplace*. San Francisco, CA: Jossey-Bass.

Neal, J., & Biberman, J. (2004). Research that matters: Helping organizations integrate spiritual values and practices. *Journal of Organizational Change Management, 17*(1), 7–10.

O'Sullivan, E. (2002). The project and vision of transformative education. In E. O'Sullivan, A. Morrell, & M. O'Connor (Eds.), *Expanding the boundaries of transformative learning* (pp. 1–12). New York, NY: Palgrave.

Palmer, P., & Zajonc, A. (2010). *The heart of higher education: A call to renewal.* San Francisco, CA: Jossey-Bass.

Taylor, E. W. (2009). Fostering transformative learning. In J. Mezirow, E. W. Taylor, & Associates (Eds.), *Transformative learning in practice: Insights from community, workplace and higher education* (pp. 3–17). San Francisco, CA: Jossey-Bass.

Tisdell, E. (2003). *Exploring spirituality and culture in adult and higher education.* San Francisco, CA: Jossey-Bass.

Tisdell, E. (2011). The wisdom of webs a-weaving: Adult education and the paradox of complexity in changing times. In E. J. Tisdell & A. L. Swartz (Eds.), *New Directions for Adult and Continuing Education: No. 131. Adult education and the pursuit of wisdom* (pp. 5–15). San Francisco, CA: Jossey-Bass.

JANET GROEN is associate professor of adult learning in the Werklund School of Education at the University of Calgary, Calgary, Canada.

COLLEEN KAWALILAK is associate dean international and associate professor of adult learning in the Werklund School of Education at the University of Calgary, Calgary, Canada.

New Directions for Adult and Continuing Education • DOI: 10.1002/ace

7

The workplace is a place where we show up as human beings, subject to human experience. People are no longer willing to leave their spirit-ness at the door. In reality, spirit-ness shows up "without permission" as a revolutionary, powerful, and transformative way of being in a world that too often supports status quo activities that are often socially unjust.

Spirit-ness at Work: Connections Between Workplace Spirituality, Transformative Learning, and Social Justice

Derise E. Tolliver

Embracing our spirituality can facilitate transformative learning and leave us more open to be social justice advocates in the workplace. However, change that emerges through transformative learning and social action is not always positively welcomed by the outside. It often occurs without official endorsement "at the edges, without permission" (Digh, 2008, p. 9). This characterization seems especially appropriate to the topic of spirituality in the workplace, where fear of imposing a religious agenda exists on the one hand and concerns that organizations might use the banner of workplace spirituality as a "technique" to coerce employees to meet the "bottom line" of profits and productivity over personal well-being, have left some people fearful about discussions of this nature. In this chapter, I attempt to address these fears and concerns as I share some thoughts about the connections between workplace spirituality, transformative learning, and social justice.

Spirituality, Spirit-ness, and Spirit

Spirituality can be an elusive as well as a contentious concept (Makgoba, April, & Al Ariss, 2014; Tolliver & Tisdell, 2006). Many definitions abound. However, the consensus that seems to emerge in the academic and popular literature is that there is no consensus for the definition of spirituality. However, there appear to be some points of convergence. In previous writings, I, along with Tisdell (Tisdell & Tolliver, 2001), discussed spirituality as it is infused in culturally grounded pedagogy supportive of transformative learning. Based on

NEW DIRECTIONS FOR ADULT AND CONTINUING EDUCATION, no. 152, Winter 2016 © 2016 Wiley Periodicals, Inc.
Published online in Wiley Online Library (wileyonlinelibrary.com) • DOI: 10.1002/ace.20214

our experiences in higher education classrooms and our reading of the scholarly literature, we described spirituality as (Tolliver & Tisdell, 2006, p. 38):

- connection to a higher power or purpose
- ourney toward wholeness
- development of an authentic identity that represents a core essence of Self construction of knowledge and meaning-making through cultural processes.

Cervantes and Parham (2005) concurred with our observation that spirituality is grounded within a cultural group's worldview. They further describe spirituality as an experience of sacredness and the existence of a force that propels one toward a purpose beyond self-centeredness. Nobles (2015), operating from an African-centered theoretical perspective, provides a distinction between spirituality and Spirit-ness. Spirit-ness refers to the condition of being Spirit. It is not a religious quality, whereas spirituality, which he defines as the quality of being spiritual, can often be confused with religion. Spirit-ness is connected to transformation and transcendence and is grounded in the central tenet of "African epistemological reflections" (Nobles, 2015, p. 6), that of Oneness with all in the universe. It represents the diunital reality of both individual experience as well as interconnectedness with others. Spirit-ness is not practicing spirituality; it is being Spirit.

Others, in their consideration of spirituality, have focused on humans "being." Bugental and Bugental (1984) emphasize Spirit as the essence and "impulsive force activating intentionality" (p. 50). They describe it as the dynamic that expresses people being the subjects of their lives rather than the objects of other forces acting upon them. Similarly, Howard (2002) described spirituality as "the essence of life itself, who we really are (our being)" (p. 232). Bugental and Bugental (1984) suggest that the uniqueness of human being-ness is the ability for transformation and actualization.

Spirituality is not the same as religion (Mohla & Aggarwal, 2014; Tolliver & Tisdell, 2006). Howard (2002) describes the distinction as spirituality being what lives are about in contrast to religion, which is a way of life. Consideration of Spirit-ness and spirituality beyond religion allows for discussion of topics and issues more inclusive and more broadly than mere doctrinal concerns. This perspective justifies consideration of the workplace as a venue for spiritual development and transformative learning.

Workplace Spirituality: Definitions, Tensions, and Possibilities

Given that people are spending more time at work and/or with work activities, and finding work to be an even more important life community, workplace spirituality emerges as an important concept to examine. Byrd (2014) describes a spiritual workplace as an "environment whereby individuals feel motivated to reach their fullest potential through creativity, emotions and intelligence" (p. 214). Based on a fairly comprehensive literature review at the time, Giacalone and Jurkiewicz (2010) considered the substantive aspects of spirituality (e.g., beliefs and relationships) and what they call the practical aspects (e.g., connection between spirituality and productivity). They presented the following as a definition of workplace spirituality:

> a framework of organizational values evidenced in the culture that promotes employees experience or transcendence through the work process, facilitating their experience of being connected to others in a way that provides the experience of completeness and joy. (p. 13).

Makgoba et al. (2014) presented a number of elements of convergence in the definitions of workplace spirituality. These include direction, wholeness, connectedness, meaning-making, integration, community, self-awareness, and living with integrity. Of particular interest is a dimension of spirituality that they describe as the transformative trend. This refers to a critical perspective that operationalizes workplace spirituality as a process and a state engaging people as change agents in their place of employment and the broader world. This dimension speaks to a spirituality "of compassion and social justice" (Makgoba et al., 2014, p. 45).

Makgoba et al. (2014) also illuminate the "pre-eminently Western" (p. 49), Eurocentric conceptualizations of workplace spirituality. One of their most important observations is that non-Western meanings, such as the African-centered considerations provided by Nobles (2015) and Honiball, Geldenhuys, and Mayer (2014), can be fruitful in the continued examination of theory, research, and applications of how workplaces can better address and support employee spiritual needs. The borrowing of African ways of knowing can be seen in the work of Nelson and Lundlin (2010) which introduced many in the Western world's business communities to the concept of Ubuntu. Ubuntu reflects the African proverb, "I am because we are, we are therefore I am" (Mbiti, 2015). This powerful concept of interconnectedness is at the heart of many definitions that have been offered for spirituality.

The central tenet of a traditional African worldview, as noted earlier, speaks to an understanding of the holistic aspects of human being-ness—the integration and harmony of mind, body, and spirit. As noted by Lips-Wiersma and Mills (2014), "Theorizing the 'whole person' is fundamental to WPS (workplace spirituality), because the very existence of WPS is based on distinct assumptions about what it is to be human" (p. 148). Spirit, from this cultural perspective, is fundamental to existence, in contrast to the privileging of the mind and rationality in Eurocentric-focused ideologies (Nobles, 2015).

From an African-centered theoretical perspective, Spirit-ness can be seen to be a central organizing principle in our lives and an essential aspect of Self (with self being a product of the individual in relationship to a group (Nobles, 2015). Thus, the concern for spirituality in the workplace is not surprising given that this is simply another arena where one shows up as a human being.

The saying that we are spiritual beings having a human experience reflects this thinking.

When Spirit-ness is not welcomed, accommodated, or "allowed" in the workplace, a number of undesired consequences may result, including lowered productivity and decreased morale. Although it is important to examine these individual and organizational outcomes, a number of scholars warn against focusing on spirituality as a technique to be manipulated by organizations to increase the bottom line of profits and efficiency (Driscoll & Wiebe, 2007; Mohla & Aggarwal, 2014). English (2013) strongly warns against the "colonization" of spirituality by corporate interests. She offers that her "opinion of this literature and experience in the workplace is that the only defensible purpose for acknowledging or cultivating the spirituality of workers ought to be for providing assistance for human flourishing, not the bottom line" (p. 27).

Some have identified compatibility issues, that is, the corporate tendency to separate church and state, as interfering with openness to conversations about spirituality (Osofo Atta, personal communication, February 20, 2016). A workplace environment that embraces this dualism "invites" an individual to leave their Spirit-ness at the door. The tension of bringing a divided, less than holistic self can impair the quality and quantity of one's work. Lips-Wiersma & Mills (2014) encourage that organizations shift from a focus on work benefits to integrating and juxtaposing spirituality with employees' work selves. They suggest that if employees are discouraged from bringing and honoring Spirit-ness, they "cannot" optimally do what they are "supposed" to do in their work and everyday lives.

Attending to Spirit-ness requires that the workplace makes space for its expression. This does not necessarily involve teaching spirituality in the workplace, although some companies may find this to be invaluable as a way to inform work when done without pushing a religious agenda (Dirkx, 2013). Sometimes physical space and/or time can be provided for prayerful expression. Proselytizing is not seen as a part of this workplace spirituality thrust, as it contradicts efforts for inclusion and respect while violating human rights and equity values (Mohla & Aggarwal, 2014). Celebration, acknowledgment, and recognition can also be critical elements of workplace spirituality.

Honiball et al. (2014) note that spirituality can become a source of coping for employees when they are dealing with challenges in the workplace. It can do this by providing a sense of meaning and higher purpose. From a spirit-centered perspective, work, like any other task, could be seen as sacred. It is in its small acts as well as in large actions that we see the possibilities of transformation and social change. This can enable transformative learning while providing opportunities to make meaningful contributions to society and to the lives of others with whom employees are in contact. Dei (2002) tells us that spirituality is a "powerful tool in resisting miseducation, domination or oppressive forces" (p. 10). It can also guide us to be agents as well as subjects of change. Again, the concepts of spirituality, transformation, and social justice become intimately related (Dei, 2002).

New Directions for Adult and Continuing Education • DOI: 10.1002/ace

Transformative Learning

The theory of transformative learning, most often associated with Mezirow (2000) and Western world thinkers in adult education, has traditionally emphasized cognitive and rational processes to address how adults make meaning of their lives. Its focus is on critical reflection in order to make more informed decisions about how to operate in the world. When faced with "disorienting dilemmas" associated with taken-for-granted perceptions and assumptions, the resolution of these are posited to help learners "gain greater control over our lives as socially responsible, clear-thinking decision makers" (Mezirow, 2000, p. 8). Mezirow suggests 10 stages in this process that could, in fact, present challenges to the existing social order in the face of inequitable and unjust situations.

Taylor (2007) has written specifically about transformative learning in the workplace, suggesting that changes in employees' perspectives can lead to creativity and productivity. The workplace environment, then, can facilitate knowledge formation, and within the context of teamwork, an increased sense of shared responsibility. Transformative learning theory in recent years has moved to increasing consideration of holistic understanding of the learning process, including spiritual dimensions of the individual.

Lancaster and Palframan (2009) suggest that the process of spirituality supports complex personal transformation, spiritual growth, and expression and is linked to values of equality and social justice. Learners can also better connect with their Spirit-ness through transformative learning experiences. Similarly, Tolliver and Tisdell (2006) posit that engaged learning in multiple dimensions of a person's life may lead to learning that is more likely to be remembered and embodied, leading to personal shifts and transformation that may inspire involvement in social justice activities. The message: we learn within our Spirit-ness and we can be transformed through learning within our Spirit-ness.

Workplace Spirituality, Transformative Learning, and Social Justice: Powerful Connections

Workplaces exist in a world where oppressive systems abound. Spirit-ness and guidance from one's spiritual values can provide an ethical and moral foundation from which to understand the way the world could be and the motivation to resist oppressions and injustice, particularly power imbalances at work (Byrd, 2014).

Embracing one's Spirit-ness can become associated with a commitment to make sure that actions are aligned with seeking the greatest good for the greatest number of people (Grills, 2002; Nobles, 2015). Injustice, unfairness, and inequity in the workplace would, then, be countered and opposed as a function of one's Spirit-ness. Consequently, to know better is to do better, which may translate to advocacy around social justice issues, particularly as they impact oneself and others at work and in the larger world (Cervantes & Parham, 2005). Workplace spirituality does not transcend the realities of power, privilege, and oppression. However, it is one's connection to transcendence that can motivate and help challenges those realities (Zimmerman, Pathikonda, Salgado, & James, 2010).

Addressing issues of spirituality may provide tools for social justice advocacy within workplace settings. For example, Shahjahan, Wagner, and Wane (2009) explore "rekindling the sacred" (p. 59) and incorporating spirituality in academic practices as ways to address issues of equity and social justice in that particular workplace setting. They suggest that spirituality is central to acts aimed at dismantling oppressions. They provide a list of tools for transformative education and learning "that is meaningful and that incorporates the authenticity of both bodies [teachers and students]" (p. 70). These authors suggest that disorienting dilemmas might occur, particularly as individuals consider ways of knowing that differ from their own. Perspective transformation can be supported in the workplace as points of congruence are highlighted and, through their Spirit-ness, employees can connect with each other and collaborate to support equity in the work environment.

In fact, spirituality in the workplace can be considered to be integrally tied to addressing issues of social justice, equity, and fairness. From an African-centered perspective, one's Spirit-ness brings with it expectations of accountability and responsibility (Dozier-Henry, 1994). This would be manifested in actions taken to ensure a socially just and equitable environment in the workplace as well as in actions to address social justice issues that are more global in nature.

A Tale of Two Workplace Experiences

The following scenarios illustrate how Spirit-ness shows up in response to social injustice and awakens a force for transformation.

Dr. C. Dr. C, a retired educator and administrator, describes her spirituality consistent with the idea of Spirit-ness (Nobles, 2015). She says that spirituality is emancipatory. It is about her humanity and how she conducts herself in everyday life. She embodies her Spirit-ness. Therefore, the workplace became another context for the expression of her Spirit-ness, with spirituality being the vehicle for her humanity. The essence of her spirituality is not for public discussion; it is grounded in values that can be deduced from her actions.

Dr. C was clear to emphasize that commitment to social justice is an important aspect of her being human. For her, social injustice is inhumanity; thus her own Spirit-ness demands that she resist acts of inhumanity. Her consciousness and awareness of sacredness and her connection to Self, others, and a Higher Power impact how she functioned within the workplace. In the face of policies and procedures that harmed others, she would be compelled to act, either by calling attention to the problematic activities to get the organization to recognize the "Spirit-killing" aspects of their policies or by actively seeking to right the perceived wrongs. Dr. C noted that her actions document that her Spirit lives, with transformative learning emerging out of this stance, allowing her to continue to grow in her meaning-making, connectedness with others, and her commitment to social justice and active involvement in making this a more just, livable world (Colin III, personal communication, March 12, 2016).

Africa Diaspora Committee. After experiencing and observing continued marginalization of the needs of adult students, staff, and faculty of African descent, several colleagues and I organized the Africa Diaspora Committee. Initially designed to provide socioemotional support in a work environment that was not always welcoming nor understanding, the committee expanded to become a vehicle that brought opportunities for transformative learning in the form of "edu-tainment" for our members, the broader university and city communities. It has been committed to self- and group empowerment and consciousness-raising in the service of positive personal and social transformation. Our membership is inclusive across job titles and geographical borders, thus "Diaspora" in our name.

Over our years of existence, we have raised money for disaster relief for Haiti and New Orleans and we sponsored symposia on social action, political education, and antiracism training. We called attention to a case of racial profiling of a young Black male staff member, accused of theft without any evidence except the report of a young colleague who said he was seen in the vicinity of the crime. Other staff, too, were observed in the vicinity, but none were subjected to multiple rounds of interrogation by security in a fishbowl room, in plain sight of others at work. Although the young man was later exonerated, the incident negatively affected all of our members in terms of morale and trust in the organization. Our efforts to address the inappropriateness of the actions taken against this staff member led to discussions with university security officers about their processes, unit-wide town hall meetings on racism, a series of focus groups to assess diversity needs, and the establishment of a standing diversity and social justice committee.

We were THE committee addressing issues of social justice and diversity before the official school committee was established. Our efforts continue to occur on the edges as we endeavor to actively shape a more just, livable world. We challenge unfair policies and situations at our school, sometimes with allies, sometimes without. We have seen our ideas and activities embraced by official school committees, then presented as their own without recognition of our pioneering work. Their events garner more widespread support and attendance from some of our colleagues. However, members of this committee engage in our efforts not for recognition and edification, but because it is purposeful and necessary. We bring our full Spirit-ness and authenticity to our events and invite that from others. In the process, we make meaning as we engage in transformative learning activities, advocate for social justice, and speak truth to power for all in our workplace.

Pulling It All Together

How can we show up, unabashedly, unashamedly, and unapologetically in our full Spirit-ness in the workplace? Some authors have noted that individuals may be fearful that showing their "sacred face" at work might lead to undesired reprisals and persecutions if theirs is seen to be outside the spiritual, religious, and even cultural norms of the status quo. It is critical to recognize and interrogate these scares and possible negative consequences of the expression of Spirit-ness.

The literature and anecdotal accounts support recognition of spirituality in the workplace, nurturing of people's Spirit-ness for positive outcomes for individuals, groups, and organizations. Here, we can expand the notion of "bottom line" to include employee satisfaction, creativity, flourishing health, motivation, and healing, in addition to the organization's efficiency and financial successes. Attending to the holistic nature of people in the workplace, for example, the integration of mind, body, and Spirit, will go a long way toward making workplaces more meaningful, relevant, and fulfilling life venues.

Spirit-ness showing up "without permission" can be a revolutionary, powerful, and transformative way of being in a world that too often supports status quo activities that are not life enhancing. Within a workplace where spirituality is honored and valued, permission is not necessary; it is presumed, nurtured, and even demanded because presence and involvement of the whole person leads to human thriving, employee satisfaction, and better personal, work, and societal outcomes.

Pursuit of social justice can take on any number of forms in the workplace. Employees might engage in activities outside their organization, such as service learning, volunteering, and giving. Inside activities informed by an individual's Spirit-ness might include advocacy for greater transparency and equity in organizational policies and procedures. This might also take the form of commitment to challenge unjust behaviors that create and perpetuate systems of privilege and oppression. Tolliver and Tisdell (2006) and Shahjahran et al. (2014) speak to this outcome as a function of the interconnectedness of spirituality and transformative learning. These scholars note that transformative learning can, in fact, be the process through which one becomes committed to the work of social justice. In our interconnectedness, we can mutually explore how to transform situations of "power over" to "power with." As noted by English (2013), "to work for spirituality means to do more than pray and meditate, it means to work for justice or to link our discussions to justice issues and support economic, social and cultural development" (p. 30). These ideas can be applied to the workplace setting.

One's Spirit-ness energizes and provides direction and guidance. That Spirit nature being nourished, nurtured, and honored can support daily consciousness and presence in the workplace. The interconnectedness with and concern for the welfare of others becomes the motivation for engaging in actions in the service of social justice. Spirituality and one's Spirit-ness become the bridge between a singular focus on "I" and the embracing of "we," the message of Ubuntu (Mbiti, 2015).

Chilisa (2012) notes that collectivity, social justice, and pluralism are implicit in the Ubuntu principle. The Rev. Dr. Martin Luther King, Jr. (1963) wrote, "I can never be what I ought to be until you are what you ought to be, and you can never be what you ought to be until I am what I ought to be . . . This is the interrelated structure of reality." The Spirit-ness of a Rev. Dr. Martin Luther King, whose workplace included the communities and streets of the United States in the late 20th century, motivated transformative learning and commitment to social justice and social action. His life exemplified the notion of spirituality that is more than a private enterprise to soothe a person's soul. In fact, the Rev. Dr. King's spiritual connection led "to a radical transformation of the individual enabling this individual to be an agent of social change in the world" (Makgoba et al., 2014, p. 44). Within the workplace environment, then, spirituality gives individuals space to consider, examine, and live into realities that give meaning to life experiences. The frame of one's Spirit-ness supports transformative learning, commitment, and involvement in social change.

Spirituality has too long existed at the margins of ideas about the workplace. Concerns that its consideration might lead to religious imposition, proselytizing, forced worship service, and more kept this important human dimension "in the closet," so to speak. However, spiritual foundation, saying yes to one's own Spirit-ness, can, in fact, be the catalyst for making work the launching pad for social action both within and outside the work organization. Commitment to a more holistic notion of human beingness has led to efforts that shift the expectations of the individual from what is to what can be, and what can be is a more just and livable world for all. Embracing Spirit-ness and spirituality in business workplaces that deal with social innovations has led to "inscaping" activities that speak to the inner life and needs of employees first, which then has translated into more efficiency, productivity, and increased loyalty among employees in companies dealing with social innovation (Nilsson & Paddock, 2014, Winter).

The marriage between workplace spirituality and transformative learning suggests that these elements together can provide powerful incentives for employees not only to "see" social justice issues but also to commit to addressing instances of social injustice within the workplace as well as in the world at large. Taking a stand such as this often requires courage and strength. Centeredness in one's Spirit-ness can often provide the motivation, energy, and support needed to do so.

We are, in our essence, Spirit (Nobles, 2015). We walk with that energy, we "be" that energy, wherever we are. Our Spirit-ness is present with us, even in the workplace. Digh (2008) comments, "Change occurs at the edges, without permission" (p. 9). So, too, are Spirit-ness and spirituality present, without permission. They help to shape how we operate at work, what and how we learn, how we experience activities, and how we make meaning in our precious lives. The question is not whether workplace spirituality exists, but rather how do we best leverage the lived experiences of humans, as spiritual beings, as our Spirit-ness guides us and our transformative learning in the workplace informs us, so that we benefit from the various bottom lines for ourselves, for our organizations, and for the world.

Conclusion

"Spirituality in the workplace is not an answer, but rather a way to ask the questions."

Martin Rutte, as quoted by Freshman, 1999, p.325

Writing this chapter was a gift for and to me. I came to the task in my full Spirit-ness, without me inviting it or it asking permission. I engaged in critical reflection of my own lived experiences of workplaces embracing or ignoring Spirit and spirituality, observations of colleagues and friends, as well as reading the scholarly and popular literature, examining what I know, what I think I know, and what I don't know. I applied my authentic cultural perspective to my understanding of the topic. I encountered some disorienting dilemmas, especially in reviewing the sometimes shadowy use of spirituality as a coercive tool to promote organizational values that do not enhance employees' experiences of a better life. Tackling these dilemmas resulted in transformative learning on my part, and a deeper understanding and commitment to advocating for social justice concerns in the context of workplace spirituality. I hope that in your reading of my writing, you will be encouraged to learn more about the connections between workplace spirituality and transformative learning and how they, together, can facilitate human thriving and effectiveness, while being challenged to commit to fully engage your authentic Spirit-ness in support of social justice in whatever workplace(s) you function.

References

Bugental, E. K., & Bugental, J. F. (1984). Dispiritedness: A new perspective on a familiar state. *Journal of Humanistic Psychology, 24*(1), 49–67.

Byrd, M. Y. (2014). Spirituality and diversity in the workforce. In M. Y. Byrd & C. L. Scott (Eds.), *Diversity in the workforce: Current issues and emerging trends* (pp. 201–217). New York, NY: Routledge.

Cervantes, J. M., & Parham, T. A. (2005). Toward a meaningful spirituality for people of color: Lessons for the counseling practitioner. *Cultural Diversity and Ethnic Minority Psychology, 11*(1), 69.

Chilisa, B. (2012). *Indigenous research methodologies*. Thousand Oaks, CA: Sage.

Dei, G. J. S. (2002). Spiritual knowing and transformative learning. *The Research Network for New Approaches to Lifelong Learning,* 4–16.

Digh, P. (2008). *Life is a verb: 37 days to wake up, be mindful, and live intentionally*. Guilford, CT: Globe Pequot Press.

Dirkx, J. M. (2013). Leaning in and leaning back at the same time. Toward a spirituality of work-related learning. *Advances in Developing Human Resources, 15*(4), 356–369.

Dozier-Henry, O. (1994). The perspective is the paradigm: The congruence of worldview and research methodology. In T. Guy, S. Colin III, & V. Sheared (Eds.), *Africentrism: perspective or paradigm? Implication for adult education, Proceedings of the African American Adult Education Research Pre-Conference, Knoxville, TN* (pp. 1–10). Athens: University of Georgia.

Driscoll, C., & Wiebe, E. (2007). Technical spirituality at work: Jacques Ellul on workplace spirituality. *Journal of Management Inquiry, 16*(4), 333–348.

English, L. M. (2013). For whose purposes? Examining the spirituality agenda in adult education. In J. Groen, D. Coholic, & J. R. Graham (Eds.), *Spirituality in social work and education: Theory, practice, and pedagogies* (pp. 17–33). Waterloo, ON: Wilfrid Laurier University Press.

Freshman, B. (1999). An exploratory analysis of definitions and applications of spirituality in the workplace. *Journal of Organizational Change Management, 12*(4), 318–327. Retrieved from http://www.choixdecarriere.com/pdf/6573/2010/Freshman1999.pdf

Giacalone, R. A., & Jurkiewicz, C. L. (2010). *Handbook of workplace spirituality and organizational performance.* Armonk, NY: ME Sharpe.

Grills, C. (2002). African-centered psychology. In T. A. Parham (Ed.), *Counseling persons of African descent* (pp. 10–23). Thousand Oaks, CA: Sage.

Honiball, G., Geldenhuys, D., & Mayer, C. H. (2014). Acknowledging others as "whole beings." Managers' perceptions of spirituality and health in the South African workplace. *International Review of Psychiatry, 26*(3), 289–301.

Howard, S. (2002). A spiritual perspective on learning in the workplace. *Journal of Managerial Psychology, 17*(33), 230–242. Retrieved from http://dx.doi.ort/10.1108/02683940210423132

King, Rev. M. L. (1963). *Letter from a Birmingham jail.* Retrieved 6 from https://www.africa.upenn.edu/Articles_Gen/Letter_Birmingham.html

Lancaster, B. L., & Palframan, J. T. (2009). Coping with major life events: The role of spirituality and self-transformation. *Mental Health, Religion and Culture, 12*(3), 257–276.

Lips-Wiersma, M., & Mills, A. J. (2014). Understanding the basic assumptions about human nature in workplace spirituality beyond the critical versus positive divide. *Journal of Management Inquiry, 23*(2), 148–161.

Makgoba, A. D. T., April, K. A., & Al Ariss, A. (2014). Understanding spirituality at work, organizations and in management. *Academy of Taiwan Business Management Review.* Retrieved from https://www.ashridge.org.uk/Media-Library/Ashridge/PDFs/Publications/Spirituality-at-work-organizations-and-in-management-ATBMR-2014_1.pdf

Mbiti, J. S. (2015). *Introduction to African religion.* Long Grove, IL: Waveland Press.

Mezirow, J. (2000). Learning to think like an adult: Core concepts of transformation theory. In J. Mezirow & Associates (Eds.), *Learning as transformation: Critical perspectives on a theory in progress* (pp. 3–33). San Francisco, CA: Jossey-Bass.

Mohla, C., & Aggarwal, S. (2014). Spiritual leadership and its potential danger at workplace: A review article. *International Journal of Organizational Behavior & Management Perspectives, 3*(3), 1076.

Nelson, B., & Lundlin, S. (2010). *Ubuntu!: An inspiring story about an African tradition of teamwork and collaboration.* New York, NY: Crown Business.

Nilsson, W., & Paddock, T. (2014, Winter). Social innovation from the inside out. *Stanford Social Innovation Review.* Retrieved from http://ssir.org/articles/entry/social_innovation_from_the_inside_out

Nobles, W. W. (2015). From Black psychology to Sakhu Djaer implications for the further development of a Pan African Black Psychology. *Journal of Black Psychology.* Retrieved from http://jbp.sagepub.com/content/early/2015/07/27/0095798415598038.full.pdf

Shahjahan, R. A., Wagner, A., & Wane, N. N. (2009). Rekindling the sacred: Toward a decolonizing pedagogy in higher education. *Journal of Thought*, *44*(1–2), 59.

Taylor, E. W. (2007). An update of transformative learning theory: A critical review of the empirical research (1999–2005). *International Journal of Lifelong Education*, *26*, 173–191.

Tisdell, E. J., & Tolliver, D. E. (2001). The role of spirituality in culturally relevant and transformative adult education. *Adult Learning*, *12*(3), 13–14.

Tolliver, D. E., & Tisdell, E. J. (2006). Engaging spirituality in the transformative higher education classroom. In E. W. Taylor (Ed.), *New Directions for Adult and Continuing Education: No. 109. Teaching for change: Fostering transformative learning in the classroom* (pp. 37–47). San Francisco, CA: Jossey-Bass.

Zimmerman, K., Pathikonda, N., Salgado, B., & James, T. (2010). *Out of the spiritual closet: organizers transforming the practice of social justice.* Oakland, CA: Movement Strategy Center.

DERISE E. TOLLIVER, PhD is a tenured associate professor at the School for New Learning, DePaul University and a licensed clinical psychologist in the state of Illinois. Her life mission is to help people remember who they truly are.

8

This chapter introduces the enlightened revelation framework, a spiritual response to social injustice. The enlightened revelation framework uses a philosophical discourse as a means to promote spiritually engaging and morally responsible workplaces.

The Enlightened Revelation: Toward a Spirit-Centered, Socially Just Workplace

Marilyn Y. Byrd

The purpose of this chapter is to contribute a social justice perspective of spirituality and recognize spirituality as a source for coping, surviving, and taking action against social injustice in the workplace. Social injustice represses an individual's right to full participation and can produce feelings of marginalization, exploitation, and powerlessness (Byrd, 2014a; Edwards & Vance, 2001). Social injustice attacks the spirit and soul and causes spirit injury, a debilitating condition that leaves a person feeling powerless and devalued (Spencer, 2006). Connecting to one's spirituality creates a form of protection, healing, and recovery (Shahjahan, 2010). At the same time, social injustices ignite a spiritual yearning for freedom (Freire, 1970). Principles of culturally relevant spirituality (Tisdell, 2002, 2004), social justice education (Adams, Bell, & Griffin, 2007), and emancipatory spirituality (Lerner, 2000) will create a foundation for the enlightened revelation framework, a philosophical and spirit-centered response to social injustice in the workplace.

Culturally Relevant Spirituality

Culturally relevant refers to the values, beliefs, norms, and customs that are foundational to one's community of affiliation or other domain that creates identity (Fowler & Hill, 2004; Tolliver & Tisdell, 2002). In the workplace, social identity groups are particularly vulnerable to social injustice and engage in spirituality as an outlet for marginalization and adversity stemming from their social identity group designation or affiliation (race, ethnicity, gender, age, disability, religion, sexual preference, etc.).

Central to the idea of cultural relevant spirituality is a sense of interconnectedness and community (Karakas, 2010). Social identity groups seek affiliation within their social group community to make sense of adverse or

New Directions for Adult and Continuing Education, no. 152, Winter 2016 © 2016 Wiley Periodicals, Inc.
Published online in Wiley Online Library (wileyonlinelibrary.com) • DOI: 10.1002/ace.20215

oppressive experiences. For example, faith in God, the power of prayer, and support from the church are considered highly favored coping resources for African American people in the struggle for civil rights and equal opportunity (Davis & McClure, 2009; Fowler & Hill, 2004; Mattis, 2000; Walker, 2009). Similarly, the Latino community maintains a sense of unity that is threatened by pressures to assimilate with the larger and dominant U.S. culture through storytelling and narratives of homeland (Gonzalez, 2009). Expressing spirituality through narratives and storytelling ignites passion to bring about change and brings to reality abstract concepts like liberation and social justice.

People experiencing social injustice stemming from their sexuality (e.g., lesbian, gay, bisexual, trans* groups) or disability engage in culturally relevant spirituality from the need to transcend traditional expectations of the "norm" and as a means to seek wholeness through community (Halkitis et al., 2009; Nosek, 1995). Grassroots movements, seminars, workshops, and blogging sites are examples of ways that gender-distinct groups seek spiritual fulfillment and engage in meaning-making processes through community affiliation. Likewise, people experiencing unequal treatment from age discrimination may need a source of well-being and acceptance of coming to the end of fruitful and rewarding career lives. Reflecting on the fullness of life, embracing the potential for continued growth, and envisioning a future of new opportunities and self-directed choices can ignite a spiritual experience (Moody, 2012).

Fundamental to a deeper understanding of culturally relevant spirituality is the process of critical reflection. Critically reflecting on disempowering experiences followed by a "coming to know" through a meaning-making process has the potential to trigger transformation and change at a higher level (Mattis, 2000; Tisdell, 2004). In the workplace, connecting to one's spirituality can become grounds for initiating transformation. Culturally relevant spirituality embodies principles of critical pedagogy, a philosophy that is derived from the notion that education and learning can be powerful vehicles for social transformation (Lauzon, 1998).

Social Justice Education and Emancipatory Learning

Social justice education is an interdisciplinary framework for analyzing the multiple ways that adversity and oppression affects learning contexts (Adams et al., 2007; Byrd & Chlup, 2012). Social justice education is a specialized instructional venue that uses structured dialogue—moving discussions beyond awareness of social injustices toward calls to action for eliminating these types of pervasive and unjust practices. Applying this framework to the workplace, individuals experiencing social injustice are provided with a set of interactive and experiential principles to deconstruct their experience for the purpose of deriving meaning. Social justice education aims to empower and enable marginalized groups to develop a sense of agency and the capacity to disrupt patterns and behaviors that are morally unjust (Bell, 2007). Therefore, workplaces are fruitful sites for emancipatory learning.

New Directions for Adult and Continuing Education • DOI: 10.1002/ace

Critical to emancipatory learning is acquiring the capacity to resist, challenge, and change oppressive sociopolitical power systems within workplace settings (Imel, 1999). Emancipatory learning occurs when individuals become empowered to take action against systems and power structures for the purpose of initiating change. In work settings, social injustice is often brought to the forefront by change agents or advocacy groups who have become spiritually energized and inspired to challenge unjust practices (Dillard, Abdur-Rashid, & Tyson, 2000; Tisdell, 1999). Transforming spiritual energy into a state of action for social change has a moral and ethical goal—particularly when the action can be perceived as the greatest good for the greatest number (Mill & Bentham, 1987).

The Enlightened Revelation Framework: An Emancipatory Perspective

Emancipatory spirituality represents an emergent perspective of workplace spirituality. Emancipatory spirituality is a philosophical approach that seeks to affirm an individual's compassion for a just society. Moreover, it is a deeply passionate and motivating experience that conveys hope (Collins, 1998). Faith in God is an exemplary form of emancipatory spirituality that invokes one's willingness to use initiative, speak out, and stand purposefully for social justice. Studies examining the lived experiences of marginalized groups have consistently found faith in God to be an inner source of strength, endurance, hope, transformation, and renewal (Byrd, 2009; Fowler & Hill, 2004; Patton & McClure, 2009). Emancipatory spirituality is based on several principles (Lerner, 2000, pp. 167–173):

- recognition of self as only a part of the whole
- cultivation of the capacity to see others as ends, not means to some other end
- affirmation of the equal worth of every human being, regardless of social affiliation
- promotion of healing and transformation of the world
- cultivation of the capacity to transcend self-interest
- ability to sustain a connection to the Spirit even through periods of adversity and pain and
- acceptance of higher forms of knowing, loving, sharing, and rejoicing that involve a release of old ways of thinking

Emancipatory spirituality gives deeper insight into the role of self in the process of being transformed and liberated from debilitating, seemingly hopeless circumstances. Furthermore, emancipatory spirituality explains how the "transformed self" provokes new ways of viewing the world. New ways of viewing the world propel one to take action not only for self but also for the good of the wider community.

Building upon emancipatory spirituality is the enlightened revelation philosophy (Byrd, 2014b). An enlightened revelation is a liberating and emancipating process of engaging one's divine beliefs in search of inner peace to endure everyday experiences that are perceived as unjust and injurious to a sense of well-being and self-worth. Limited attention has been given to the role of spirituality as a force for confronting unjust practices and systems that create feelings of marginalization and disregard for human dignity in the workplace (Hicks, 2003; Schaeffer & Mattis, 2012). An enlightened revelation is spirit driven and empowers those having an oppressive experience to improve their circumstances. It is a principles-driven philosophy that focuses on equal respect and dignity in the workplace.

Given that "social justice is a concept that originates in philosophical discourse" (Jost & Kay, 2010, p. 1122), the enlightened revelation uses a philosophical as well as spiritual approach for bringing about social justice and social change. Fundamental to the enlightened revelation framework is the universality of moral actions, or the belief that everyone has a moral right to be treated equally and with respect. The universality of moral actions is a basic assumption of Kant's categorical imperative philosophy, which poses the following questions:

- What do I know?
- What ought I do?
- What can I hope?

These questions acknowledge the quest for answers to a disempowering situation or event and at the same time acknowledges there is a desired state that will bring about a "coming to know" for improved conditions and a better state of well-being.

The enlightened revelation framework assumes a relationship between an agent group and a target group. Bell and Griffin (2007) explain this relationship as the power of an agent group, through embedded institutional norms, to define the reality of a target group and as a result, the target group ultimately conforms to the agent group's ideology. When a target group member first encounters a negative experience or "event" enacted by an agent group, affective stressors are placed on the target group member's physical and mental well-being, which limits the ability to function effectively in professional roles (Byrne, Morton, & Dahling, 2011). Emotional and affective stressors cause feelings of alienation, isolation, exclusion from social networks, and/or lack of support in performing work (Byrd, 2014b). Encountering these types of adverse experiences ignites the process of descriptive thinking (Ingram & Walters, 2007). During descriptive thinking, "surface information is most apparent and readily recalled and/or repeated" (p. 28); however, detailed information needed to attach meaning and ultimately learning is limited.

Next, a target group member seeks to understand the event and engages in a "coming to know" through critical reflection. Critical reflection is a process of

Figure 8.1. Enlightened Revelation: A Spiritually Relevant Framework.

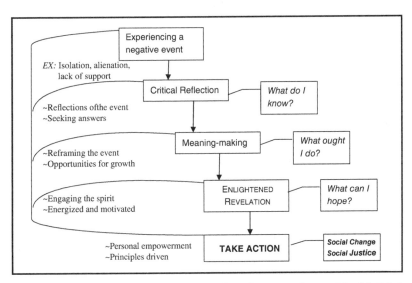

Source: Copyright (2014) from "Spirituality in the workforce" by M. Y. Byrd. In M. Y. Byrd & C. L. Scott (Eds.) *Diversity in the workforce diversity: Current issues and emerging trends*. Reproduced by permission of Taylor and Francis Group, LLC, a division of Informa pic.

self-consciousness that unveils the social structures and practices that situates a person in negative and adverse circumstances (Ingram & Walters, 2007). After critically reflecting on the event, a target group member goes through a meaning-making process by minimizing the impact on personal well-being and reframing the event as an opportunity for growth and development (Tisdell, 1999, 2000, 2002). Spirituality can help locate an event within a grander plan than at first realized and the event takes on a deeper and more powerful meaning (Gall et al., 2005).

Finally, meaning-making leads to a state of enlightened revelation, a liberating and emancipating state that is motivating, energizing, and purposeful. Enlightened revelation is the engaging of one's spiritual or divine beliefs in hopes of a future state that transcends the present circumstances. Therefore, an enlightened revelation is not only spiritually relevant; it is morally relevant as a force for social justice and social change. Figure 8.1 is an illustration of the enlightened revelation framework that explains a spiritually relevant social justice outcome.

Another fundamental outcome of an enlightened revelation is the capacity to feel hope. Hope is a powerful spiritual resource for coping during times of despair (Lazarus, 1999). A basic element of hope is that some event or future occurrence will bring about a change that will improve current circumstances that are perceived as psychologically damaging and are beyond control.

Hope and faith in God has emerged consistently in studies as a dominant response to social injustice in oppressive workplace experiences (Brown-McManus, 2012; Byrd, 2009; Lathon, 2005; Mattis, 2000; Ritter-Seltzer, 2009; Walker, 2009). The salient themes in these studies reveal how spirituality is a driving force in coping with social oppression and how in the "midst of fear and confusion, amid turmoil and uncertainty, appropriate actions and responses will somehow be revealed" (Dym & Hutson, 2005, p. 77). The sustaining power of spirituality emerging from personal experiences of marginalization and domination has enabled educators to reach across the traditional educational boundaries to evoke hope and encourage action against social injustice (hooks, 2003). The enlightened revelation framework represents a morally as well as a culturally relevant basis for scholars, practitioners, organizational consultants, and social justice advocates who are seeking ways to promote spiritually engaging and morally responsible workplace settings.

New Horizons: Giving Voice and Expanding the Paradigm

Until lions speak, tales of the hunt will glorify the hunter . . .

Old African proverb

The goal of this chapter has been to bring to light emergent perspectives of spirituality in the workplace and recognize principles of social justice as an outcome. The enlightened revelation framework that was introduced is a spiritually grounded, philosophical framework for contributing to discourse on ways that individuals, particularly those marginalized by their social identity group, are empowered and become potential agents of change or social justice advocates in their workplace. One means of empowerment is giving voice. Giving voice means to "speak the truth of consciousness and experiences . . . voice lingers close to the true and the real and because of this proximity has become almost as a mirror of the soul, the essence of the self" (Jackson & Mazzei, 2009, p. 1). Giving voice to an injustice is a fundamental element of personal agency for making social change happen (Ashby, 2011). In addition, giving voice is the first step toward actions that can lead to social justice (Choo & Ferree, 2010). Finally, giving voice is a moral sense of duty to respond not only to the individual having the oppressive experience but also to others similarly oppressed.

Call to Action. Giving voice alone is not sufficient for bringing about social change in the workplace. Allies for social justice are necessary actors in the social change process (Edwards, 2006). Allies are members of a privileged group motivated by their own spirituality or moral duty to respond. Furthermore, as a member of the privileged group, allies have the power to challenge and influence others and thereby change or transform unjust systems (Hardiman, Jackson, & Griffin, 2007).

New Directions for Adult and Continuing Education • DOI: 10.1002/ace

Allies can actively contribute to the transformation of unjust systems by proposing and actively pursuing the establishment of social justice educational programs in the workplace where social justice goals are not as clearly labeled as such. Social justice goals can be enacted by establishing employee resource groups whereby individuals can create community with others similarly socially located and by creating workforce social justice councils, an internal task force with the authority to take appropriate action on issues of social injustice (Byrd, 2014a). Both of these venues are spaces for giving voice.

Eliminating social injustice, however, is predicated on sustained dialogue (Saunders, 2012). Sustained dialogue is a systematic, ongoing change process with the goal of transforming relationships. Central to the process is the assumption that in order to address social injustices and engage in conversations to eradicate these problems, it is necessary to examine the associated relationships and not just the concrete, presenting problem itself. The goal for continued and persistent dialogue is dismantling barriers and building relationships.

Paradigm Shift. Collectively, this volume has shifted and expanded the discourse on spirituality to the workplace. In that context engaging spirituality can promote organizational social justice (Byrd, 2012). Organizational social justice is the "ideology that organizations operating through a representing agent seek to achieve a state whereby all individuals feel included, accepted, and respected, and whereby human dignity as well as equality are practiced and upheld" (p. 120). An integrative perspective of spirituality, social justice education, and emancipatory learning may be the keys to better explain, understand, and "restore individual and collective humanity" (Edwards, 2006, p. 52) to the workplace. The enlightened revelation philosophical framework introduced in this chapter is a beginning step toward integrating these concepts and applying the benefits to the workplace.

The connection the world's waiting for is to connect the hunger for spirituality with passion for social change. Because spirituality, when it isn't disciplined by social justice, in an affluent society, becomes narcissistic.
Jim Wallis, interview with Michal Lumsden, March 10, 2005

References

Adams, M., Bell, L. A., & Griffin, P. (2007). *Teaching for diversity and social justice*. New York: Routledge.

Ashby, C. A. (2011). Whose "voice" is it anyway?: Giving voice and qualitative research involving individuals that type to communicate. *Disability Studies Quarterly, 31*(4). Retrieved from http://dsq-sds.org/article/view/1723

Bell, L. A. (2007). Theoretical foundations for social justice education. In M. Adams, L. A. Bell, & P. Griffin (Eds.), *Teaching for diversity and social justice* (2nd ed., pp. 4–14). New York: Routledge.

Bell, L. A., & Griffin, P. (2007). Designing social justice courses. In M. Adams, L. A. Bell, & P. Griffin (Eds.), *Teaching for diversity and social justice* (2nd ed., pp. 68–87). New York: Routledge.

Brown-McManus, K. C. (2012). *We walk by faith, not by sight: An inquiry of spirituality and career development of black women leaders in academe* (Doctoral dissertation). Retrieved from ProQuest Dissertations and Theses. (Order No. 3545629).

Byrd, M. (2009). Telling our stories: If we don't tell them they won't be told. *Advances in Developing Human Resources, 11*(5), 582–605.

Byrd, M. (2012). Theorizing leadership of demographically diverse leaders. In M. Paludi (Ed.), *Managing diversity in today's workplace: Strategies for employees and employers (Women and careers in management)* (pp. 103–124). Santa Barbara, CA: Praeger (ABC-CLIO).

Byrd, M. Y. (2014a). Re-conceptualizing and re-visioning diversity in the workforce: Toward a social justice paradigm. In M. Y. Byrd & C. L. Scott (Eds.), *Diversity in the workforce: Current issues and emerging trends* (pp. 334–346). New York: Routledge.

Byrd, M. Y. (2014b). Spirituality in the workforce. In M. Y. Byrd & C. L. Scott (Eds.), *Diversity in the workforce: Current issues and emerging trends* (pp. 201–218). New York: Routledge.

Byrd, M., & Chlup, D. (2012). Theorizing African American women's learning and development in predominantly white organizations: Expanding the conversation on adult learning theories. In C. Scott & M. Byrd (Eds.), *Handbook of research on workforce diversity in a global society: Technologies and concepts* (pp. 38–55), Hershey, PA: IGI Global.

Byrne, C. J., Morton, D. M., & Dahling, J. J. (2011). Spirituality, religion, and emotional labor in the workplace. *Journal of Management, Spirituality & Religion, 8*(4), 299–315.

Choo, H. Y., & Ferree, M. M. (2010). Practicing intersectionality in sociological research: A critical analysis of inclusions, interactions, and institutions in the study of inequalities. *Sociological Theory, 28*(2), 129–149.

Collins, P. (1998). *Fighting words: Black women and the search for justice.* Minneapolis, MN: University of Minnesota Press.

Davis, L. P., & McClure, M. (2009). Strength in the spirit: African American college women and spiritual coping mechanisms. *Journal of Negro Education, 78*(1), 42–54.

Dillard, C. B., Abdur-Rashid, D. I., & Tyson, C. A. (2000). My soul is a witness: Affirming pedagogies of the spirit. *International Journal of Qualitative Studies in Education, 13*(5), 447–462.

Dym, B., & Hutson, H. (2005). *Leadership in nonprofit organizations.* Thousand Oaks, CA: Sage.

Edwards, K. E. (2006). Aspiring social justice ally identity development: A conceptual model. *NASPA Journal, 43*(4), 39–60.

Edwards, P., & Vance, S. (2001). Teaching social justice through legal writing. *Legal Writing, 7*, 63–86.

Fowler, D. N., & Hill, H. M. (2004). Social support and spirituality as culturally relevant factors in coping among African American women survivors of partner abuse. *Violence Against Women, 10*(11), 1267–1282. doi:10.1177/1077801204269001.

Freire, P. (1970). *Pedagogy of the oppressed.* New York, NY: Continuum.

Gall, T. L., Charbonneau, C., Clarke, N. H., Grant, K., Joseph, A., & Shouldice, L. (2005). Understanding the nature and role of spirituality in relation to coping and health: A conceptual framework. *Canadian Psychology, 46*(2), 88–104.

Gonzalez, M. A. (2009). *Embracing Latina spirituality: A woman's perspective.* Cincinnati: OH. St. Anthony Messenger Press.

Halkitis, P. N., Mattis, J. S., Sahadath, J. K., Massie, D., Ladyzhenskaya, L., Pitrelli, K., ... Cowie, S. E. (2009). The meanings and manifestations of religion and spirituality among lesbian, gay, bisexual, and transgender adults. *Journal of Adult Development, 16*(4), 250–262.

Hardiman, R., Jackson, B., & Griffin, P. (2007). Conceptual foundations for social justice education. In M. Adams, L. A. Bell, & P. Griffin (Eds.), *Teaching for diversity and social justice* (2nd ed., pp. 35–66). New York: Routledge.

Hicks, D. A. (2003). *Religion and the workplace: Pluralism, spirituality, leadership.* Cambridge: Cambridge University Press.

hooks, B. (2003). *Teaching community: A pedagogy of hope.* New York: Routledge.

Imel, S. (1999). *How emancipatory is adult learning?* (Myths and Realities No. 6). Columbus: ERIC Clearinghouse on Adult, Career, and Vocational Education, Ohio State University. Retrieved from ERIC database. (ED436663)

Ingram, I. L., & Walters, T. S. (2007). A critical reflection model to teach diversity and social justice. *Journal of Praxis in Multicultural Education, 2*(1), 23–41.

Jackson, A. Y., & Mazzei, L. A. (2009). *Voice in qualitative inquiry. Challenging conventional, interpretive, and critical conceptions in qualitative research.* London: Routledge.

Jost, J., & Kay, A. C. (2010). Social justice: History, theory, and research. In S. T. Fiske, D. Gilbert, & G. Lindzey (Eds.), *Handbook of social psychology* (5th ed., Vol. 2, pp. 1122–1165). Hoboken, NJ: Wiley.

Karakas, F. (2010). Spirituality and performance in organizations: A literature review. *Journal of Business Ethics, 94*(1), 89–106.

Lathon, E. B. (2005). *"I cried out and none but Jesus heard." Prophetic pedagogy: The spirituality and religious lives of three nineteenth century African-American women* (Doctoral dissertation). Retrieved from ProQuest Dissertations and Theses. (Order No. 3199740).

Lauzon, A. C. (1998). Adult Education and the human journey: An evolutionary perspective. *International Journal of Lifelong Education, 17*(2), 131–145.

Lazarus, R. S. (1999). Hope: An emotion and a vital coping resource against despair. *Social Research, 66*(2), 653–678.

Lerner, M. (2000). *Spirit matters.* Charlottesville, VA: Hampton Roads Publishing.

Lumsden, M. (2005). God's politics: An interview with Jim Wallis. Retrieved from http://www.motherjones.com/politics/2005/03/gods-politics-interview-jim-wallis

Mattis, J. S. (2000). African American women's definitions of spirituality and religiosity. *Journal of Black Psychology, 26*(1), 101–122. doi:10.1177/0095798400026001006.

Mill, J. S., & Bentham, J. (1987). *Utilitarianism and other essays* (A. Ryan, Ed.). New York: Penguin Group.

Moody, H. R. (2012). *Religion, spirituality, and aging: A social work perspective.* New York: Routledge.

Nosek, M. A. (1995). The defining light of Vedanta: Personal reflections on spirituality and disability. *Rehabilitation Education, 9*(2–3), 171–182.

Patton, L. D., & McClure, M. (2009). Strength in the spirit: African American college women and spiritual coping mechanisms. *Journal of Negro Education, 78*(1), 42–54.

Ritter-Seltzer, B. D. (2009). *Exploring how spirituality shapes workplace ethical perceptions among African American women* (Doctoral dissertation). Retrieved from ProQuest Dissertations and Theses. (Order No. 3348173).

Saunders, H. H. (2012). Sustained dialogue in conflicts: Transformation and change. New York: Palgrave McMillan.

Schaeffer, C. B., & Mattis, J. S. (2012). Diversity, religiosity, and spirituality in the workplace. *Journal of Management, Spirituality, & Religion, 9*(4), 317–333.

Shahjahan, R. A. (2010). Toward a spiritual praxis: The role of spirituality among faculty of color teaching for social justice. *Review of Higher Education, 33*(4), 473–512.

Spencer, E. B. (2006). Spiritual politics: Politicizing the Black church tradition in anti-colonial praxis. In G. J. S. Dei & A. Kempf (Eds.), *Anti-colonialism and education: The politics of resistance* (pp. 107–127). Rotterdam: Sense.

Tisdell, E. J. (Ed.). (1999). *New Directions for Adult and Continuing Education: No. 84. The spiritual dimension of adult development.* San Francisco, CA: Jossey-Bass.

Tisdell, E. J. (2000). Spirituality and emancipatory adult education in women adult educators for social change. *Adult Education Quarterly, 50*(4), 308–336.

Tisdell, E. J. (2002). Spiritual development and cultural context in the lives of women adult educators for social change. *Journal of Adult Development, 9*(2), 127–140.

Tisdell, E. J. (2004). The connection of spirituality to culturally responsive teaching in higher education. *Spirituality in Higher Education Newsletter, 1*(4). Retrieved from http://spirituality.ucla.edu/docs/newsletters/1/Tisdell.pdf

Tolliver, D., & Tisdell, E. J. (2002). Bridging across disciplines: Understanding the connections between cultural identity, spirituality and sociopolitical development in teaching for transformation. In J. M. Pettitt & R. P. Francis (Eds.), *Proceedings of the 43rd Adult Education Research Conference* (pp. 391–396). Raleigh: North Carolina State University.

Walker, S. A. (2009). Reflections on leadership from the perspective of an African American woman of faith. *Advances in Developing Human Resources, 11*(5), 646–656.

MARILYN Y. BYRD, PhD, is assistant professor Department of Human Relations, University of Oklahoma, Norman, OK.

INDEX

Practical facilitation techniques tailored to the adult brain

Facilitating Learning with the Adult Brain in Mind explains how the brain works and how to help adults learn, develop, and perform more effectively in various settings. Recent neurobiological discoveries have challenged long-held assumptions that logical, rational thought is the preeminent approach to knowing. Rather, feelings and emotions are essential for meaningful learning to occur in the embodied brain. Using stories, metaphors, and engaging illustrations to illuminate technical ideas, Taylor and Marienau synthesize relevant trends in neuroscience, cognitive science, and philosophy of mind.

This book provides facilitators of adult learning and development a much-needed resource of tested approaches plus the science behind their effectiveness.

- Appreciate the fundamental role of experience in adult learning

- Understand how metaphor and analogy spark curiosity and creativity

- Alleviate adult anxieties that impede learning

- Acquire tools and approaches that foster adult learning and development

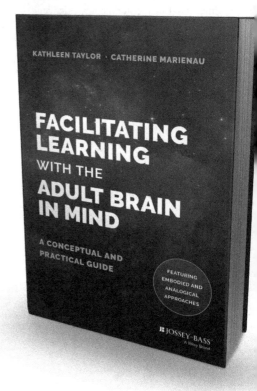

 Also available as an e-book.

JB JOSSEY-BASS
A Wiley Brand

Jossey-Bass is a registered trademark of John Wiley & Sons, Inc.

NEW DIRECTIONS FOR ADULT AND CONTINUING EDUCATION

ORDER FORM SUBSCRIPTION AND SINGLE ISSUES

DISCOUNTED BACK ISSUES:

Use this form to receive 20% off all back issues of *New Directions for Adult and Continuing Education*. All single issues priced at **$23.20** (normally $29.00)

TITLE	ISSUE NO.	ISBN
_____	_____	_____
_____	_____	_____
_____	_____	_____

Call 1-800-835-6770 or see mailing instructions below. When calling, mention the promotional code JBNND to receive your discount. For a complete list of issues, please visit www.wiley.com/WileyCDA/WileyTitle/productCd-ACE.html

SUBSCRIPTIONS: (1 YEAR, 4 ISSUES)

☐ New Order   ☐ Renewal

U.S.	☐ Individual: $89	☐ Institutional: $356
CANADA/MEXICO	☐ Individual: $89	☐ Institutional: $398
ALL OTHERS	☐ Individual: $113	☐ Institutional: $434

Call 1-800-835-6770 or see mailing and pricing instructions below.
Online subscriptions are available at www.onlinelibrary.wiley.com

ORDER TOTALS:

Issue / Subscription Amount: $ _____

Shipping Amount: $ _____
(for single issues only – subscription prices include shipping)

Total Amount: $ _____

SHIPPING CHARGES:

First Item	$6.00
Each Add'l Item	$2.00

(No sales tax for U.S. subscriptions. Canadian residents, add GST for subscription orders. Individual rate subscriptions must be paid by personal check or credit card. Individual rate subscriptions may not be resold as library copies.)

BILLING & SHIPPING INFORMATION:

☐ **PAYMENT ENCLOSED:** *(U.S. check or money order only. All payments must be in U.S. dollars.)*

☐ **CREDIT CARD:** ☐ VISA ☐ MC ☐ AMEX

Card number _____Exp. Date_____

Card Holder Name_____Card Issue # _____

Signature _____Day Phone_____

☐ **BILL ME:** *(U.S. institutional orders only. Purchase order required.)*

Purchase order # _____
Federal Tax ID 13559302 • GST 89102-8052

Name_____

Address_____

Phone_____ E-mail_____

Copy or detach page and send to: **John Wiley & Sons, Inc. / Jossey Bass**
PO Box 55381
Boston, MA 02205-9850

PROMO JBNND